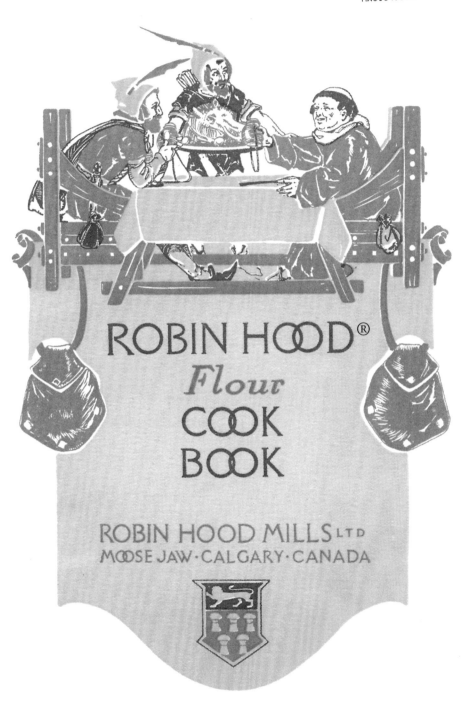

ROBIN HOOD® *Flour* COOK BOOK

ROBIN HOOD MILLS LTD
MOOSE JAW · CALGARY · CANADA

Historical Notes by Elizabeth Driver

whitecap

SPRING WHEAT
98 LBS
ROBIN HOOD
FLOUR
THE ROBIN HOOD MILLS
LIMITED
98 LBS
ROBIN HOOD

Whitecap Books

Elizabeth Driver would like to thank Jim Anderson, the owner of Anderbooks, Winnipeg, Manitoba, which specializes in the sale of historic cookbooks, for securing the original copy from which this edition was made.

Printed in Canada

National Library of Canada Cataloguing in Publication Data
Rorer, Sarah Tyson, 1849–1937
Robin Hood cook book / recipes by Mrs. Rorer ; historical notes, Elizabeth Driver.

(Classic Canadian cookbook series)
Includes index.
ISBN 1-55285-405-1

1. Cookery, Canadian. I. Robin Hood Multifoods Limited. II. Title. III. Series.
TX715.6.R64 2003 641.5 C2003-911058-3

The publisher acknowledges the support of the Canada Council for the Arts and the Cultural Services Branch of the Government of British Columbia for our publishing program. We acknowledge the financial support of the Government of Canada through the Book Publishing Industry Development Program for our publishing activities.

Please note that the ingredients, methods and cooking times listed in this book are consistent with the kitchen appliances and techniques that were in use in 1915. Current equipment and supplies may produce different results that are inconsistent with contemporary food safety theories.

Visit our website at www.whitecap.ca.

Table of Contents

The recipes in this Cook Book were prepared and written for our special use by Mrs. S. T. Rorer, are copyrighted, and are published by permission of her publishers, Arnold & Company, Philadelphia, Pa.

Bulman Bros. Limited, Printers, Winnipeg, Man.

Introductory & Foreword

This is not an ordinary advertising Cook Book. When the matter of a Robin Hood Cook Book was first proposed, we felt that there were already in the market too many of the ordinary advertising cook books, most of them being poorly printed on cheap paper, containing a conglomeration of recipes compiled by some printer or advertising agency, and all of more or less doubtful value.

We felt that there was a place for a Cook Book which would be worthy of the Robin Hood name, and which would in every respect, like all of the Robin Hood products, be **different.** Nearly two years of preparatory work and $10,000.00 in money was spent on the first edition of this book. If published and distributed through book stores in the regular way, it could not be sold at retail for less than $1.25 to $1.50 per copy.

No pains have been spared to make the Robin Hood Cook Book the finest example of modern printing. Note particularly the seven beautiful three-color process plates showing the Robin Hood products in their natural color. This is the first time this expensive process has been used in any cook book in Canada. There are in addition about forty illustrations, also in three colors, showing scenes from the life of Robin Hood. One of the leading American artists, Mr. Moen, has been engaged for the past year gathering material and drawing this beautiful series of illustrations.

Foreword Continued

Our aim was to make the book not merely artistic and beautiful, but practical. After considerable investigation we found that the best recognized authority on the culinary art was Sarah Tyson Rorer, for many years one of the editors of the Ladies' Home Journal, and author of many books on cooking, all of them recognized as standard and authoritative.

We found Mrs. Rorer was under contract with her publishers, Arnold & Co., of Philadelphia. After considerable negotiation she secured their permission to undertake the work of compiling especially for this book the recipes contained therein. The fee paid her for this service was a handsome one, but we had the satisfaction of knowing that the recipes would be complete and perfect in every respect.

Mrs. Rorer's recipes for baking Robin Hood flour and for cooking Robin Hood Porridge Oats were made with the Robin Hood product.

In testing our Robin Hood Flour she writes, "I found the flour excellent —in fact I am afraid it has quite spoiled me for the flour I can buy in my neighborhood" (Philadelphia, Pa.). She writes further—"The Robin Hood Porridge Oats have been pronounced by everybody—delicious, and I find it very good."

It is needless to state that money could not buy her testimonial. The above is surely an appreciation by an expert.

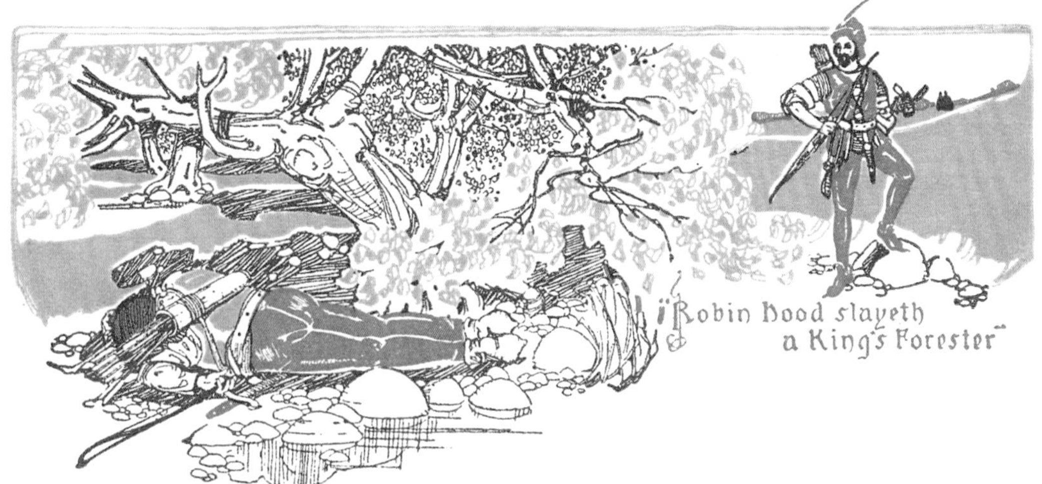
"Robin Hood slayeth
a King's Forester"

Soups

One of the most important points in correct soup making is to use the best materials. Meat contains many constituents, but in soup making we are especially concerned in the nitrogenous *fibrin*, *gelatin*, *albumin* and *fat*. Gelatin is dissolved by slow heat, and solidifies when cold. Albumin coagulates under the influence of heat, comes to the surface in the form of a brown scum and is skimmed off; this robs the soup of this part of its nourishment, but makes it perfectly clear.

Clear Stock

Buy a shin or leg of beef; have the butcher saw them into lengths of four inches. Remove the meat from the bone, put the bones in the bottom of the kettle and the meat on top. If you wish a dark, brilliant, amber, tasty soup, run the bones into a hot oven until they are slightly toasted. Cover the meat and bones with five quarts of cold water, cover the kettle, bring the water to boiling point and simmer at a temperature of 180° Fahr. for three hours. The point is this—it must not boil rapidly, nor must it fall much below 180° Fahr., or the consommé will taste of the suet. Skim the soup carefully and add one onion (with twelve cloves stuck in it), one carrot, one turnip and a few celery tops (chopped), two bay leaves, parsley and salt; cover the kettle closely and let it cook at the same temperature for one hour longer. Strain through a sieve and stand it aside to cool; when cold, remove all the fat from the surface, and it is ready for use, either as plain consommé, bouillon or other clear soups. Boiled barley and rice added to hot stock make nice dinner soups.

Remove the marrow from the bones, cut it into slices and put it aside for toasted marrow on bread; this forms a very nice luncheon dish. The meat may be made into jellied beef or into curry, or it may be sliced and served with rich brown sauce for dinner. As the water has drawn out the flavorings of the meat, it must be made into a highly seasoned dish or it is not palatable. If the soup be made properly, it will be a perfectly clear jelly, and can be served in summer as cold consommé, cold beef soup or cold bouillon, or beef jelly.

Bean Soup

One pint of turtle or navy beans.
Two quarts of boiling water.
One quart of clear soup or stock.
Two hard boiled eggs.
One lemon.
Salt and pepper to taste.
If you use wine, one gill.

Wash the beans in cold water and soak them over night; in the morning drain, cover with boiling water and boil rapidly ten minutes. Drain, return them to the kettle, add the two quarts of boiling water and boil slowly until they are tender, about two hours, or in a fireless cooker over night. Press them through a sieve. Wash the kettle, return the soup, add a quart of good stock, salt and pepper, and boil twenty minutes. Slice the hard boiled eggs and lemon, put them in the tureen and pour over the soup. Serve.

If wine is used, put it in the tureen with the lemon and egg.

The turtle beans are black, the navy are white, but one recipe will answer for both these and split peas and lentils.

If the soup settles, you have used too coarse a sieve.

Vegetable Soup

Two quarts of clear soup or stock.
One quart of boiling water.
One carrot.
One turnip.
One white potato.
One ear of corn.
One cupful of peas.
One tomato.
One tablespoonful of rice.

Corn, peas and tomatoes may be fresh or canned.

Put the water in a soup kettle. Cut the vegetables into pieces of uniform size. Put the carrot and turnip in the water, cook slowly one hour, then add all the other vegetables; add the stock, salt and pepper to taste, bring to a boil, cook until the vegetables are tender, and serve.

Soup Julienne

Make the same as vegetable soup, cut the vegetables into long, thin strips and add at least a head of lettuce, shredded.

Sago or Tapioca Soup

One quart of stock.
One tablespoonful of sago or pearled tapioca.

Wash the tapioca or sago, boil it in the seasoned stock until transparent, and serve.

Clear Tomato Soup

One quart of stewed or canned tomatoes.
One pint of stock.
One teaspoonful of salt.
A dash of red pepper.
One tablespoonful of grated onion.
A suspicion of mace.
One tablespoonful of butter.

Put all the ingredients, except butter, into a saucepan, bring to boiling point, boil five minutes and strain through a fine sieve. Stir in the butter and send at once to the table.

This may be converted into a very elegant soup by putting a tablespoonful of whipped cream on the top of each cup of soup; garnish the cream with a dusting of paprika.

Consommé à la Colbert

Heat plain consommé or clear soup. Poach one egg for each person, drop them into the tureen, pour over the soup and send to the table. In dishing, ladle one egg into each soup plate.

Macaroni and Vermicelli

Simply add boiled vermicelli or macaroni, cut into one-inch lengths, into the hot consommé.

Turkish Soup

One quart of stock or clear soup.
Half cupful of boiled rice.
The yolks of two eggs.
One tablespoonful of cream.
Salt and pepper to taste.

Throw the boiled rice into the consommé, boil ten minutes, press through a sieve and return the soup to the kettle. Add the salt and pepper; when this is hot add the yolks of the eggs and the cream, beaten together. Take immediately from the fire and serve in cups. The soup must not boil after the eggs are added, or it will curdle.

Ox Tail Soup

Two ox tails.
Two quarts of clear soup or stock.
One teaspoonful of caramel.
Salt and pepper to taste.
If you use wine, two tablespoonfuls of sherry.

Wash and wipe the ox tails, cut them into pieces at the joints, put them into a baking pan, run them into a hot oven until they are nicely browned; lift them from the fat and put them at once into the hot consommé. Add the seasoning, and simmer until the tails are tender, about one hour; add the caramel and serve. If the stock should become reduced until there is too little soup, add at serving time an extra pint of hot stock.

Every Day Stock

In every household there is sufficient material for ordinary soups without buying a shin or a leg. For instance, the carcase of a chicken, the centre bone from a steak, the clean ribs from the roast, the bones from the leg of mutton, must all do duty in the family stock pot. Save the bones on Sunday and Monday; on Tuesday, when perhaps there is a long fire for ironing, put them into a soup kettle, cover with cold water, bring to a boil and simmer gently two hours. Add the seasonings the same as for clear stock, an onion with twelve cloves, two bay leaves, and celery tops or celery seed; simmer one hour longer and strain. This stock may be used for any ordinary every-day soup.

I rarely ever buy meat for soup, and find it quite easy to have a different soup almost every day in the month.

Bouillon for Parties and Germans

Two pounds of lean beef from the round.
One and one-half quarts of cold water.
One small onion.
One bay leaf.
A sprig of parsley.
The outside pieces of a root of celery, or
Half teaspoonful of celery seed.

Free the meat from all fat and gristle, and chop it fine; put it in a soup kettle, with the water, bay leaf, parsley, onion and celery. Cover the kettle closely, put it on the back of the fire or over a slow fire for at least two hours; then place it over a good fire and bring it quickly to a boil. Strain, return it to the soup kettle, add the whites of two eggs beaten with a little cold water, a tablespoonful of lemon juice, a teaspoonful of salt and a saltspoonful of black pepper. Boil rapidly five minutes and strain through two thicknesses of cheese cloth. If you use a flannel bag for straining, make sure it is scalded and perfectly free from odor. This is ready to serve, and may be served plain, colored slightly with caramel, or with lemon or wine.

Mock Turtle Soup

One unskinned calf's head.
One onion.
Twelve cloves.
Five quarts of cold water.
A saltspoonful of celery seed.
One carrot.
Two bay leaves.
Salt and pepper to taste.

Singe and thoroughly wash the calf's head. With a sharp knife remove the skin from the head; take out the tongue and the brains and put them aside for another dish. Put the bones of the head in a soup kettle and put the skin on top; cover with the water and simmer gently four hours until the skin is perfectly tender; then remove it, add the onion and cloves, the carrot sliced, and all the seasonings, and simmer gently one hour longer. When the skin is cold, cut it into pieces one inch square. Strain the soup and stand it aside until cold; remove the fat. At serving time reheat the soup with the blocks of skin. If it is not clear, clarify it before adding the skin. If you have more skin than is needed for the soup, it may be served as calf's head turtle fashion, or calf's head à la poulette, or calf's head with sauce vinaigrette; the tongue and the brains will be cooked separately for these dishes.

Chicken Broth

Chicken broth takes the place of a clear consommé or bouillon; it represents a clear chicken soup. Purchase a fowl two years old, have it carefully dressed, put it into the soup kettle with five quarts of cold water, and proceed as you would for clear soup or stock. When the chicken is tender it may be removed and used with egg sauce, as boiled chicken. The broth will be strained and put aside to form the basis of noodle soup, soup à la Reine, Bellevue bouillon or chicken jelly.

Noodle Soup

Cook two ounces of noodles in one quart of chicken broth until tender; season with salt and pepper.

Soup à la Reine

One cupful of chopped white meat of chicken.
One quart of chicken broth.
Two tablespoonfuls of rice.
One tablespoonful of butter.
Two tablespoonfuls of Robin Hood flour.
A teaspoonful of salt.
A dash of pepper.
Half cupful of milk.

Put the chopped meat, rice and broth into a soup kettle, simmer gently for a half hour, add the seasoning and the butter and flour rubbed together; when this boils and slightly thickens, add the milk, and when hot, serve.

Bellevue Bouillon

Heat equal quantities of good clam bouillon and chicken bouillon. Mix, season to taste, pour into bouillon cups, put a tablespoonful of whipped cream on top of each cup, garnish with a dusting of paprika and send to the table. This is one of the nicest of luncheon soups.

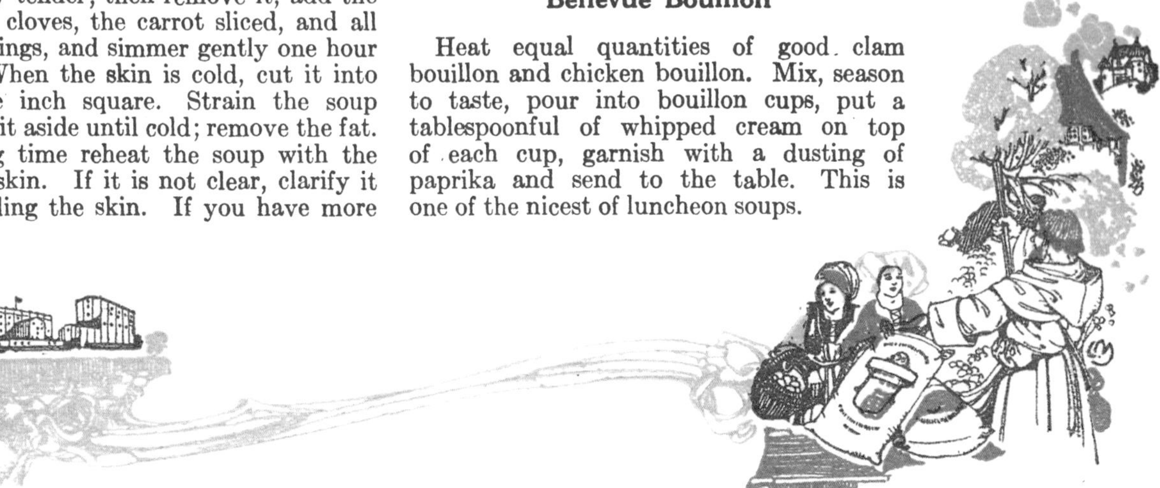

SOUPS MAIGRE

Oyster Soup

One solid pint of oysters.
One quart of milk.
One dozen whole peppercorns.
One tablespoonful of butter.
One level tablespoonful of cornstarch.
One teaspoonful of salt.
One saltspoonful of black pepper.

Drain the oysters in a colander. Boil the liquor, skim and strain it; add to it a half pint of cold water and the oysters; boil and skim again. Put the milk in a double boiler, add the cornstarch moistened in a little cold milk; when this begins to thicken, add the butter, salt and pepper; turn it quickly in the kettle with the oysters. Heat and serve. Do not boil or the soup will curdle.

Cream of Pea Soup

One pint of shelled peas, or
One can.
One quart of milk.
One tablespoonful of butter.
Two tablespoonfuls of Robin Hood flour.
One teaspoonful of salt.
A saltspoonful of pepper.

If the peas are raw, boil them until tender in just as little water as possible, and press them through a colander; if canned, simply press the whole through a colander. Put the milk in a double boiler, add the butter and flour rubbed together, and when smooth and slightly thickened add the peas; add the salt and pepper, and when smoking hot serve with small squares of toasted bread.

This recipe will answer also for asparagus and young beans, or limas.

Cream of Potato Soup

One pound, or four medium sized potatoes.
A saltspoonful of celery seed.
One bay leaf.
One quart of milk.
One tablespoonful of butter.
Two tablespoonfuls of Robin Hood flour.

Cover the potatoes with boiling water, bring to a boil, drain and throw the water away. Put them back into the saucepan with one pint of boiling water, the celery seed and bay leaf; cover and cook until the potatoes are tender, and press the whole through a colander. Rub the butter and flour together, add it to the hot milk in the double boiler; when it thickens add it slowly to the mashed potatoes; add the salt and pepper. Put a sieve or gravy strainer over the top of the double boiler and pass the soup through it; heat just a moment and serve.

This is one of the nicest of the cream soups.

Cream of Tomato Soup

One pint of tomatoes.
One quart of milk.
One tablespoonful of butter.
Two tablespoonfuls of Robin Hood flour.
One teaspoonful of salt.
One saltspoonful of pepper.
Half teaspoonful of baking soda.
A saltspoonful of ground mace.
One slice of onion.

Put the tomato, onion, mace and pepper into a saucepan and cook slowly five minutes. Put the milk in a double boiler, add the butter and flour, rubbed together, and stir until smooth and slightly thickened. Strain the tomatoes into the soup tureen, which had been previously heated with hot water, add to them the soda, stir a minute, turn in hastily the hot milk and send at once to the table. This soup will never curdle if made carefully according to this recipe.

Cream of Celery Soup

Three roots of celery.
One quart of milk.
One tablespoonful of butter.
Two tablespoonfuls of Robin Hood flour.
One pint of water.
Salt and pepper to taste.
A piece of onion the size of a silver quarter.

Wash the celery and cut it into small pieces. Cover it with the water and boil thirty minutes; then press it through a colander. Put the milk on to boil in a farina boiler, add to it the water and celery that was passed through the colander, also the onion. Rub the butter and flour together, and stir into the boiling soup, and stir constantly until it thickens. Add salt and pepper and serve at once.

"Robin Hood
meeteth Little John

Fish

Fish

Fish, to be wholesome and eatable, must be perfectly fresh. One can easily distinguish a fresh fish by the clearness of the eyes, the bright red color of the gills, the firmness of the flesh and the stiff condition of the scales. All fish, both fresh and salt water, should be cooked as soon as possible after they are taken from the water. Scale, split and wash the fish, take out the intestines quickly without soaking, removing the smallest atom of blood; dry it with a soft cloth and put it at once into a cold place. If necessary to keep it over night, dust it lightly with salt on the flesh side. White-fleshed fish, such as cod, halibut, haddock and whitefish, are more easily kept than the oily fish like mackerel, sturgeon and salmon.

To Boil a Fish

Clean and wash the fish. Without a fish kettle, lay it on a piece of cheese cloth and put it down into a deep baking pan of boiling water; add a tablespoonful of vinegar or lemon juice, a slice of onion, a teaspoonful of salt and a sprig of parsley. Simmer gently ten minutes to each pound of fish. When done, lift the fish in the cheese cloth, drain, turn it on to a heated platter and garnish with slices of lemon and parsley. Serve with sauce Hollandaise or plain drawn butter. If the fish breaks or the skin is disfigured you have boiled it too long or too hard.

All cold boiled fish left over may be utilized in salads, croquettes, or à la creme.

This general rule will answer for the boiling of all kinds of fish.

Fish à la Creme

One pint of cold cooked fish.
One pint of milk.
Two level tablespoonfuls of butter.
Three level tablespoonfuls of Robin Hood flour.
A teaspoonful of onion juice.
A tablespoonful of chopped parsley.
A teaspoonful of salt.
A saltspoonful of black pepper.

Flake the fish. Rub the butter and flour together, add the milk and stir until boiling; add the salt and all the other seasonings, then add the fish and stir carefully so as not to break the flakes; when hot it is ready to serve. Or it may be turned into a baking dish, covered with crumbs and browned in the oven; or it may be served in individual dishes browned in the same way.

Fish Croquettes

One pint of cold cooked fish.
Half pint of milk.
Half cupful of soft bread crumbs.
Two tablespoonfuls of butter.
Three tablespoonfuls of Robin Hood flour.
One tablespoonful of chopped parsley.
One teaspoonful of salt.
A dash of cayenne.

Rub the butter and flour together and add the milk; stir over the fire until you have a thick, smooth paste; take from the fire and add the bread crumbs and all the seasoning. Put in the fish and mix as carefully as possible, then stand the mixture aside until perfectly cold; then form into cylinders four inches long. Roll them first in an egg beaten with a tablespoonful of water, then in bread or cracker crumbs, and fry in deep hot fat. Serve on a napkin garnished with parsley.

This recipe will answer for all kinds of fish croquettes.

To Boil Salt Cod at High Altitudes

Wash the fish through several cold waters, cover with fresh cold water and soak all day At night wash it again, cut it into convenient pieces, put it into the fireless cooker, cover with cold water, add a slice of onion, a saltspoonful of black pepper, a bay leaf and a sprig of parsley. Bring to boiling point, boil five minutes, and put it into the fireless cooker over night. Next morning it will, of course, be lukewarm. Remove it from the water and put it aside until nearly serving time; then reheat over the fire and serve with either tomato or white sauce.

For cod fish balls or picked cod with cream sauce, the first cooking will be exactly the same.

To Fry Fish

Perch, brook trout, catfish, smelts—in fact all small fish—are best fried. They should be well cleaned, washed in cold water and immediately wiped dry, inside and out. Use oil—cotton-seed or peanut, as convenient—or use lard mixed with a small amount of dripping. Never use butter, as it has a tendency to soften the flesh of fish. Dust the fish with salt and pepper, dip them first in beaten egg, then in bread crumbs, and fry them in deep hot fat, about 340° Fahr.

To sauté fish, dust with salt, pepper and flour; cook in a small quantity of dripping or lard.

To Broil Fish

This is the nicest way of cooking large fish—lake trout, slices of salmon or whitefish. Dust the fish with salt and pepper and brush it with butter; put it in a wire double broiler, expose the flesh side to the fire and broil slowly until it is a golden brown. Turn, and broil the skin side carefully, without burning. It is well to elevate the broiler at least six inches above the fire. When the fish is done, loosen it carefully from the broiler so as not to break the brown outside. Turn it at once on to a heated platter, brush with melted butter and send at once to the table. A fish weighing four pounds will take about a half hour to broil.

Baked Fish

After the fish has been thoroughly scaled, open down the belly, wash and wipe it dry; stuff it with seasoned bread crumbs and sew it up with soft twine. Put the fish in a baking pan; cut deep gashes with a sharp knife on one side and put a thin strip of bacon in each gash. Cover the bottom of the baking pan with water, dust the fish with salt, pepper and flour, and bake fifteen minutes to each pound in a quick oven basting every ten minutes. If the water evaporates, add more water. When done, dish the fish on a heated platter, garnish with quarters of lemons, fried potato balls and parsley. Serve with plain tomato sauce or sauce Hollandaise.

Planked Fish

Secure a hard wood plank just a little smaller than your oven; have it perfectly smooth on both sides; braced at the ends, if you like, it will last a life time.

In Front of a Wood Fire

Rear the plank in front of the fire until it is very hot. Have the fish split down the back, wash and wipe it quickly, put it, skin side down, on the hot plank, folding over the thin part, dust it with salt and pepper, brush it with butter, stand it in front of the fire and let it cook three-quarters of an hour, basting every now and then with melted butter. To keep the fish in place, drive a couple of tacks in the head portion. Serve on the plank, garnished with lemons and parsley. Pass cucumber or lettuce salad, and creamed potatoes.

To Plank Under the Gas Stove

Rub the board with salt, put it underneath the gas lights until very hot, put on the fish, skin side down, dust it with salt and pepper, brush it with butter, and cook under the gas flame for fifteen minutes. Have ready a quart of good hot mashed potatoes, season them with salt and pepper, add a half cupful of hot milk, beat until light, put them in a pastry bag with a star tube and press them through, making roses around the entire board. Put this back in the oven until the potatoes are a golden brown; this should take fifteen minutes longer. Garnish the fish with parsley and lemon, and send to the table on the board.

In a coal stove oven, simply heat the board on the upper shelf, cook the fish twenty-five minutes on the plank, garnish it with potatoes, and when the potatoes are brown send it to the table.

Robin Hood turneth butcher"

Meats

Baked Ribs of Beef with Yorkshire Pudding

Remove the ribs, roll the meat and tie it into shape with twine; do not use wooden skewers. Place the meat in a baking pan and dust it lightly with pepper. Add a teaspoonful of salt to a cupful of water and pour this into the pan. Put at once into a very hot oven, basting three times in the first ten minutes. As soon as the meat is nicely browned, reduce the heat of the oven, and bake fifteen minutes to each pound of meat. One hour before the meat is done, make the pudding. Pour nearly all the dripping from under the meat into another baking pan, turn the pudding into it and bake one hour.

Pudding

Three eggs.
One pint of milk.
Half teaspoonful of salt.
Eight level tablespoonfuls of Robin Hood flour.
A saltspoonful of pepper.

Beat the eggs, whites and yolks together, until light; add them to the milk; add these gradually to the flour, stirring all the while. When smooth, strain through a fine sieve, add the salt and pepper, and bake. To serve, cut into squares and place them around the meat on the platter.

A Pot Roast

In high altitudes this must be done in a fireless cooker. Trim off the rough parts from a nice piece of brisket, or shoulder, or round of beef. Place it in a kettle over a good fire, brown it quickly on one side, turn and brown it on the other; then add a pint of boiling water, cover the kettle and boil for forty minutes. Then dust the meat with salt and pepper and add another quart of boiling water. Put this into the fireless cooker over night. At serving time simply reheat and send to the table. If you are without a fireless cooker, this must be cooked slowly, at a temperature of 200° Fahr. fifteen minutes to every pound of beef. Serve with brown sauce made from the fat in the pan.

Rolled Beef Steak

A slice from the round, or
One flank steak.
One cupful of stale bread crumbs.
One tablespoonful of chopped parsley.
One tablespoonful of butter or suet.
One teaspoonful of sweet marjoram.
Half teaspoonful of salt.
A saltspoonful of pepper.

Mix the bread crumbs, parsley, marjoram, salt and pepper together, and add the suet or butter, melted. Spread this over the steak, roll tightly and tie with twine; put it in a baking pan with a few pieces of suet, add a half cupful of water and bake in a quick oven one hour. Serve with brown sauce made in the pan.

Cannelon of Beef

One pound of uncooked beef, chopped fine.
One egg.
Half cupful of bread crumbs.
One teaspoonful of salt.
A saltspoonful of pepper.
If you like, a teaspoonful of grated onion.

Put the meat through the meat chopper, add all the other ingredients, adding the egg at last. Form it into a roll six inches long and about four inches in diameter, and wrap it in a piece of brown paper, slightly oiled. Put it in a baking pan and bake in a quick oven an hour, basting over the paper once or twice with melted suet. When done, remove the paper, place the roll in the centre of a heated platter and pour over brown or tomato sauce. This is one of the nicest of the cheap meat dishes.

Jellied Meat

Chop cold soup meat or ordinary boiled beef rather fine. To each quart of this meat allow:

Half pint of stock or clear soup.
A tablespoonful of gelatin.
Two hard boiled eggs.
One medium sized onion.
A teaspoonful of salt.
A saltspoonful of pepper.

Cut the eggs into thin slices. Put the gelatin in the cold stock and heat it gently until the gelatin is dissolved. Garnish the bottom of a square bread pan with the eggs; add the seasoning to the meat, and pack it on top of the eggs. If you have any egg left, put the slices on top of the meat. Pour over the stock and gelatin, and stand aside to harden. Serve cut into slices, with an accompaniment of potato or cabbage salad.

Beef Steak Pie

One quart of cold cooked meat cut into dice.
Two slices of bacon cut into small pieces.
Half pint of stock.
A tablespoonful of butter.
A tablespoonful of Robin Hood flour.
Six medium sized potatoes cut into dice.
A teaspoonful of salt.
A saltspoonful of pepper.

Line a baking dish with plain paste. Boil the potato dice five minutes and drain. Put a layer of meat in the bottom of the baking dish on top of the paste, then a layer of potatoes, then a few pieces of bacon, then a dusting of salt and pepper, then another layer of meat, and so continue until all the ingredients are used. Put the butter in a saucepan, add the flour, add the stock, boil, add a teaspoonful of browning, pour this over the meat, cover with plain paste, making a small hole in the centre of the pie, and bake in a moderately quick oven one hour.

Steak Stanley

Two pounds of beef from the round.
Four bananas.
Half pint of milk.
Two tablespoonfuls of butter.
Two tablespoonfuls of Robin Hood flour.
Two tablespoonfuls of grated horse-radish.
One teaspoonful of salt.

Peel the bananas, break them into halves, put them in a baking pan, add a tablespoonful of melted butter, one of sugar, and bake three-quarters of an hour. Put the raw meat through the meat grinder, add the salt, and form into eight cakes. Put them in a dry pan in the oven to cook slowly for a half hour. Rub the butter and flour together, add the milk, stir until boiling, add a half teaspoonful of salt and the horseradish; stand over hot water until the meat is cooked. When the bananas are soft, put them for a minute over a quick fire until they are slightly browned. Pour the sauce in the bottom of a meat platter, stand the steaks neatly in the sauce, put a half of a banana on top of each steak and send at once to the table.

This is one of the nicest of the chopped meat dishes.

Indian Steak

Two pounds of beef from the round.
A cupful of stewed tomatoes.
A small can of Spanish sweet peppers.
Two teaspoonfuls of curry powder.
One onion.
One teaspoonful of salt.
The juice of half a lemon.
Two tablespoonfuls of butter.
Two tablespoonfuls of Robin Hood flour.

Add the salt to the meat and form into eight cakes. Put the butter in a saucepan, add the onion, chopped, shake until the onion is soft, not brown; add the curry powder and the flour, mix, and add the tomato, and peppers pressed through a sieve. Stir until boiling, and stand it over hot water. Broil or pan the steaks quickly, or you may cook them in the oven, and when nearly done, lift them into the sauce; cover the saucepan and steep or cook slowly fifteen minutes. Serve with this dish boiled rice, and if you like, chutney.

Tournedos

One pound of round of beef.
Quarter pound of bacon.
Two tablespoonfuls of Robin Hood flour.
A teaspoonful of browning or kitchen bouquet.
Half teaspoonful of salt.
A dash of pepper.

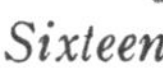

Put the bacon in a saucepan and try out all the fat; lift the bacon and put it on a dish to dry; it must be curled and crisp. Cut the meat into squares of one inch, throw them into this hot bacon fat, and shake and turn until every piece is nicely browned; add the flour and one pint of stock or water, stir until boiling, add the seasoning and the browning, cover the saucepan and cook slowly an hour and a half, or in a fireless cooker three hours. When ready to serve, cover the bottom of a platter with either fried mush, fried farina or toast, dish over the tournedos, garnish the dish with the bacon and send to the table.

Braised Leg of Mutton

One leg of mutton.
One carrot.
One onion.
One turnip.
Half teaspoonful of celery seed.
Four whole cloves.
A teaspoonful of salt.
A saltspoonful of pepper.

Wipe the leg with a damp towel. Slice the vegetables, put them in the bottom of a baking pan, put the leg on top, add one quart of boiling water, cover the pan and put it into a quick oven for a half hour. Baste the leg, reduce the heat of the oven slightly, and bake, covered, fifteen minutes to each pound of meat. When done, dish the leg on a heated platter and garnish the bone with a paper frill. Put two tablespoonfuls of butter in an ordinary saucepan and stir it over the fire until a nice brown, then add two tablespoonfuls of flour and stir again until the flour is brown; add a pint of the water from the baking pan; when boiling, add a tablespoonful of Worcestershire sauce if you have it, and if necessary a little more salt and pepper. Pour this over the leg, garnish the dish with squares of toast and send it to the table. Serve with it potatoes or boiled rice and currant jelly.

This is one of the nicest of the mutton dishes, and may easily be cooked over night in a fireless cooker.

Curry of Mutton

One pint of cold cooked mutton cut into blocks.
One tablespoonful of suet or butter.
One tablespoonful of Robin Hood flour.
Two teaspoonfuls of curry powder.
Half teaspoonful of salt.
One large onion.
Half pint of boiling water.

Put the butter or suet into a saucepan; when melted, add the onion, chopped; shake until the onion is soft, not brown, then add the curry powder, the flour, and then the water; stir until boiling and add the salt and meat. Cover the saucepan and sort of steep the meat in the sauce for fifteen or twenty minutes. Remove the lid, and if you have it, add a tablespoonful of lemon juice. Have ready a half pound of nicely boiled rice; heap the rice in the centre of a platter, pour over the curry and send to the table. To be absolutely correct, you should pass with this, chutney and baked bananas; many curry eaters, however, prefer the bananas served raw; they eat them with the curry as they would eat bread.

Shepherd's Pie

One quart of blocks of cold cooked mutton.
One pint of cold boiled potatoes cut into dice.
Half pint of stock or water.
One tablespoonful of butter.
A teaspoonful of salt.
A saltspoonful of pepper.

Boil four good sized potatoes; when they are done, drain, mash, add a half cupful of hot milk and sufficient flour to make a soft dough; season it with salt and pepper. Cut the cold boiled potatoes into dice. Put a layer of the blocks of mutton in the bottom of a baking dish, then a layer of potatoes, salt and pepper; continue until you have used the ingredients. Cut the butter into bits and put it over the top; take the boiled potato mixture and pat it out on a baking board with your hands, lift it carefully to the top of the pie, making a hole in the centre, brush it with a little milk and bake in a moderate oven one hour.

Veal Loaf

Three pounds of lean veal.
One cupful of bread crumbs.
One teaspoonful of salt.
One tablespoonful of onion juice.
Two eggs.
Half teaspoonful of pepper.
Half teaspoonful of sage.
Half teaspoonful of ground cloves.

Half teaspoonful of ground allspice.
Half pound of lean ham.

Put the veal and ham through a meat grinder, add all the seasoning, and the eggs, one at a time; break them into the meat, and mix thoroughly; press in a square bread pan to mould. Turn this into a baking pan, add a half cupful of water and bake in a slow oven two and a half hours, basting once or twice with a little melted butter. Serve cold, cut into thin slices.

Veal Ragout

Meats
Continued

Two necks of veal.
One quart of stock or water.
Three level tablespoonfuls of Robin Hood flour.
Four level tablespoonfuls of dripping.
One onion.
One carrot.
One teaspoonful of salt.
One saltspoonful of pepper.

Put the dripping in a stewing pan, add the onion and carrot, chopped, shake until they are slightly brown, add the meat, cover and simmer gently for a half hour. Lift the lid, add the flour to the fat, mix, add the water and the seasoning, stew over the fire one hour, or cook in a fireless cooker two hours.

The yolk of an egg may be added to this at the last minute, or you may add a teaspoonful of browning or kitchen bouquet.

Creamed Sweetbreads

Wash a pair of sweetbreads, throw them into boiling water and cook slowly for three-quarters of an hour; cool them quickly, remove the membrane and pick them apart. Rub together two level tablespoonfuls of butter and two of flour, add a half pint of milk, stir until boiling, add a half teaspoonful of salt, a saltspoonful of pepper, and if you have them, a half can of mushrooms, sliced. Add the sweetbreads, stand the saucepan over boiling water, cover, and let them heat for twenty minutes.

Ham Baked in Cider

Wash a small ham and soak it over night in cold water. Next morning mix together a cupful and a half of flour and enough water to make a tough dough. Dust the flesh side of the ham with pepper, a half teaspoonful of ground cinnamon, half a teaspoonful of ginger, then put over a tablespoonful of grated onion. Roll the dough out and put it on top of the seasoning, and fasten it down nicely to the skin. Put the ham, skin side down, in a baking pan, fill the pan with cider and bake slowly three or four hours; in a fireless cooker put it aside over night. To serve, remove the dough, which is now a hard crust, and the skin; trim the bone of the ham neatly, put it in a dry baking pan, fat side up, dust the fat thickly with bread crumbs, garnish it nicely by sticking in whole cloves, and bake in a quick oven until a nice brown. Boil the cider that is in the pan until reduced to the consistency of a good sauce; remove the fat and strain the sauce into a boat. Garnish the bone of the ham with a quill of paper and send it to the table.

This is the most delicious way of cooking ham, and it is good both hot and cold.

A salt beef's tongue may be cooked after this same rule, omitting, of course, the covering with the paste. The tongue will be boiled for two hours, the skin removed, and then cooked in cider.

To Boil a Ham

Wash the ham well in cold water. To do this thoroughly, you should use a small scrubbing-brush. Put it into a large boiler filled with cold water, add a blade of mace, six cloves, and a bay leaf. Place it over a slow fire, that it may heat gradually. It should not come to boil for at least two hours. Then skim carefully and simmer gently fifteen minutes to every pound, from the time it begins to simmer. When done, allow it to cool in the liquor in which it was boiled. Then remove the rind carefully without cutting the fat. Brush it over with beaten egg, and sprinkle with dried bread crumbs; place in a quick oven for about fifteen minutes to brown. Serve it cold, garnished with parsley. Ornament the shank bone with a paper frill.

OR TO SERVE HOT

Remove the skin as soon as it is done, and while yet hot, brush it over with beaten egg, sprinkle with dried bread crumbs, and put in the oven to brown and crisp. When brown, dish; trim the shank bone with frill of paper, garnish the edge of the dish with parsley and vegetable flowers and serve with it asparagus, peas, or cauliflower.

Robin meeteth a stranger in scarlet

Poultry & Game

Chicken in Jelly

One fowl.
Half box of gelatin.
One teaspoonful of salt.
One onion.
One lemon.
Ten drops of Tobasco sauce.
Three quarts of cold water.
Four hard boiled eggs.

Clean the chicken, cover it in a soup kettle with the cold water, boil rapidly for five minutes; if you have a fireless cooker, put it aside over night; if not, cook slowly for three hours. Remove the chicken and put it aside until cold. Add the onion and all the seasoning to the water, boil rapidly twenty minutes, strain and stand it aside until perfectly cold. When cold remove every particle of fat, return the stock to the kettle, add the gelatin and stir slowly until it comes to boiling point, add the juice of the lemon and strain through two thicknesses of cheese cloth. Dip a square bread pan or mould into cold water. Slice the hard boiled eggs, garnish the mould with the eggs, cut the chicken into blocks and fill the mould.

Pour over the liquid jelly and stand it aside over night.

This is a beautiful dish to serve for afternoon receptions, or Sunday night suppers, or evening collations. Pass with it a boat of mayonnaise dressing.

Chicken Croquettes

Chop sufficient cold chicken to make a pint.
Two tablespoonfuls of butter.
Three tablespoonfuls of Robin Hood flour.
Half pint of milk.
A saltspoonful of grated nutmeg.
A tablespoonful of chopped parsley.
A level teaspoonful of salt.
A teaspoonful of onion juice.
A saltspoonful of pepper.
A dash of cayenne.

Rub the butter and flour together, add the milk, stir over the fire until thick and smooth. Add all the seasoning to the meat, then mix it in the thick white sauce and turn out to cool; when cold, form into cylinders or pyramids, dip in egg beaten with a tablespoonful of water, roll thoroughly in bread or cracker crumbs, and fry in deep hot fat.

This recipe will answer for all kinds of meat croquettes.

Serve chicken croquettes with peas; veal croquettes with mayonnaise of celery; beef croquettes with tomato sauce; lamb croquettes with peas.

Panned Chicken

Divide a year-old chicken into joints as you would for stewing; wash and wipe quickly, put the pieces in a baking pan, cover the top with five or six slices of thin bacon, dust with pepper and run into a quick oven to bake for a half hour. Cool the oven to a medium heat, add a half cupful of stock or water, and cook the chicken until tender, about forty-five minutes longer; dish neatly. Add two tablespoonfuls of Robin Hood flour to the fat in the pan, and a half pint of water, stock or milk—milk preferable; stir until boiling, add a half teaspoonful of salt, and a half teaspoonful of paprika if you have it. Pour this over the chicken, garnish the dish with small potato or farina croquettes and serve.

French Method of Roasting Turkey

Singe and draw the turkey. Boil and shell one quart of chestnuts. Put one pound of ham through a meat grinder. Mash the chestnuts through a colander, add the ham, a quarter of a grated nutmeg and a saltspoonful of white pepper; put this stuffing, hot, into the turkey, sew up the vents and truss it into shape. Put it, back down, in a baking pan, brush the breast with melted butter, put a teaspoonful of salt in the pan, add a half cupful of water, and put it into a hot oven. Brown it on all sides quickly, then roast it slowly about two and a half to three hours. An eight-pound turkey will take two and a half hours, a larger turkey three hours. Baste the turkey every twenty minutes. When the turkey is done, remove the trussing and dish. Add to the pan two tablespoonfuls of Robin Hood flour, mix thoroughly with the fat in the pan, add a cupful and a half of milk, stir until boiling, add twenty-five fat oysters, or a can of mushrooms, chopped fine. Stir until the gills of the oysters are curled. Serve the sauce into a sauce boat. Serve with the turkey stuffed potatoes or potato soufflé, or plain boiled rice, and baked onions.

Boudins of Turkey

One pint of cold cooked turkey chopped fine.
Half cupful of stock or water.
Half cupful of soft bread crumbs, or
Half cupful of cold cooked Robin Hood farina.
One teaspoonful of salt.
A saltspoonful of pepper.
Two eggs.
If you have it, a tablespoonful of chopped parsley.

Add the bread crumbs to the stock or water; if you use farina in the place of bread crumbs add milk in the place of stock or water. Stir this over the fire until hot, add the meat and all the seasoning, and when well mixed add the eggs, beaten. Fill the mixture into small custard cups, stand the cups in a pan of water and bake in the oven until they are "set," that is, until they will resist pressure in the centre. Make a cream sauce, pour it in the bottom of the platter, turn out the boudins and send to the table.

This recipe will answer for Chicken or Veal Boudins, simply substituting these meats for turkey.

Turkey Cylinders

One pint of mashed potatoes.
One pint of chopped cooked turkey.
One egg.
One teaspoonful of onion juice.
One teaspoonful of salt.
One saltspoonful of pepper.

If the potatoes are cold, put them in a saucepan and stir them over the fire until they are slightly heated; take from the fire and add the egg, beaten, and all the other ingredients. When cool, form into cylinders, dip in an egg beaten with a tablespoonful of water, roll in bread crumbs and fry in deep hot fat. Serve with cream sauce and peas.

Chicken, veal or lamb may be substituted for turkey.

Potted Birds

Half dozen birds or pigeons.
Quarter pound of bacon.
Two level tablespoonfuls of Robin Hood flour.
One pint of stock or water.
One tablespoonful of Worcestershire sauce.
One bay leaf.
One onion.
A teaspoonful of salt.
A dash of pepper.

Singe, draw and truss the birds. Put the bacon in a shallow frying pan and try out all the fat. Dust the birds thickly with the flour and put them, breast down, in the hot fat; turn until they are nicely brown, then lift them to a stewing pan or a casserole mould. Add a tablespoonful of flour to the fat that is in the pan, then the stock or water, salt, pepper, bay leaf, onion, sliced, and the Worcestershire sauce; when this is boiling pour it over the birds, cover the saucepan or casserole mould, and cook in an oven two hours; in a fireless cooker four hours. Serve with either boiled rice or potato puff.

GAME

Venison Cutlets

Trim the cutlets nicely, put them in a casserole mould and cover with a marinade made as follows:

To each pound of venison allow:
Four tablespoonfuls of good vinegar.
Four tablespoonfuls of claret.
One small onion, sliced.
Four whole cloves.
A blade of mace.

Bring this to boiling point and pour it over the cutlets; stand them aside over night. Next day lift the cutlets carefully and broil them over a quick fire. Serve with melted butter and currant jelly.

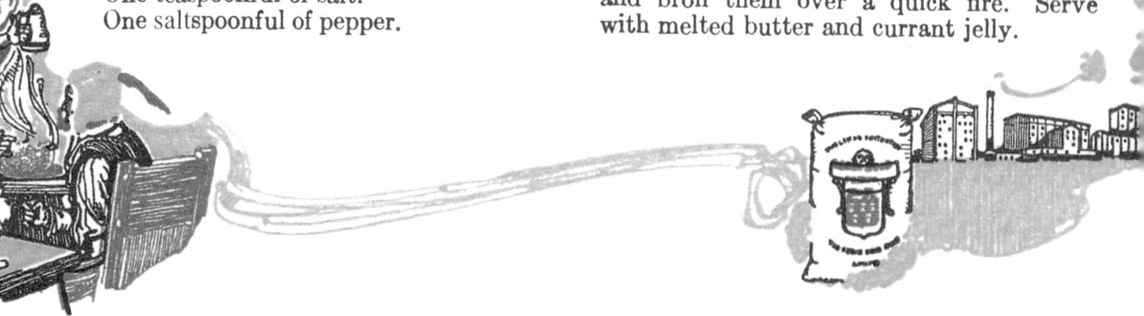

Haunch of Venison Roasted

Wipe the venison well with a towel dipped in warm water. Leave the hoof and four or five inches of skin or hair on the lower part of the leg. Lard the haunch thickly with salt pork. If you have no larding-needle, make slight incisions with a small knife, about an inch and a half apart, and put a small piece of salt pork in each incision. It may be roasted without larding, but as the meat is naturally dry, it is certainly a great improvement. Fold a piece of coarse muslin into three or four thicknesses, wide enough to cover the hoof and hair. Dip this in cold water, and bind it around the hoof and hair, tie, envelop this in several thicknesses of buttered letter paper and tie tightly. This is to prevent the hair and hoof from changing color. If your haunch is large, the cloth may require a second or third wetting. Now place it before a brisk fire, or in a very hot oven, and roast fifteen minutes to every pound, basting every ten minutes at first with melted butter, and afterwards with its own drippings. When half done season with a teaspoonful of salt and a few dashes of black pepper. When done, unwrap the hoof and dish. Add two tablespoonfuls of Robin Hood flour to the fat in the pan in which it was roasted, stir until brown, add one pint of good stock, stir constantly until it boils; take from the fire, add one tablespoonful of currant jelly and one of sherry, season with salt and pepper to taste. Serve in a boat. Currant jelly and water-cress should accompany this dish.

Saddle of Venison Roasted

Saddle and shoulder may be roasted the same as the haunch. As they cannot so well be larded, cover with several thicknesses of buttered paper while roasting, to prevent the juices from drying out.

Panned Rabbit

Clean and cut into halves as directed. Place in a baking pan, spread lavishly with butter, dust with salt and pepper, and bake in a quick oven one hour, basting every ten minutes. When done, lay on a heated dish. Add one tablespoonful of flour to the fat in the pan; mix well; add a half-pint of boiling water, stir until it boils, add salt and pepper to taste, pour it over and around the rabbit, and it is ready to serve.

Roast Wild Duck

Pick, draw, and singe the same as chicken. Wipe them inside and out with a damp towel. Do not wash them unless you break the gall or intestines, as it greatly destroys the flavor. If they have a fishy odor, rub the breast lightly with a piece of onion, and put three or four cranberries (uncooked) in the duck before cooking it. Tuck back the wings and truss the legs down close to the body. Put the cranberries and a piece of butter the size of a walnut in each duck. Place them in a baking pan, add one teaspoonful of salt and a quarter cup of boiling water to the pan, baste them well with melted butter, put them into a very hot oven, and bake forty-five minutes, if wanted rare; one hour, if well done; basting with their own gravy every five minutes. When done serve with gravy from the pan poured over them. Wild ducks are much better when not stuffed; but if stuffing is preferred, potato is best.

Serve currant jelly and green peas with them.

Wild Goose

A wild goose may be selected and cooked precisely the same as a wild duck.

Roast Partridge

Pick and draw the same as chicken. Wipe them carefully, inside and out, with a wet towel; then dry them. Do not wash unless you wish to spoil them. Now tuck the wings back, and fasten the legs up to the sides of the body with a small skewer, so that when the bird is on its back the legs stand up, not down towards the rump, as you truss a chicken. Lard them thickly over the breast (this may be omitted, but they are not so good), place them in a baking-pan or before a good fire, baste with melted butter at first and afterwards with their own gravy; dredge with salt and pepper when half done. Roast three-quarters of an hour, if liked rare; if well done one hour. Serve on squares of toast, with the gravy in the pan poured around them. Garnish with parsley.

Bear Meat

Bear meat is best roasted. It may be treated the same as pork, cooking twenty minutes to every pound.

Bear Steaks

Bear steaks may be cooked in a chafing-dish, the same as venison steaks, omitting the currant jelly.

Smothered Prairie Chicken

Split prairie chickens down the back, wipe with a damp cloth, put them in a baking pan, skin side up; put over the breast of each a slice of bacon, put in the pan a half cupful of stock or water, dust the birds with pepper, cover with another pan and bake one and a half hours in a moderately quick oven, basting several times. Serve these with a brown sauce made in the pan, garnish the dish with small pieces of broiled ham and serve with them French fried potatoes.

Game Pie

For this any of the birds mentioned in the preceding recipes may be used. We will use partridges. Bone the partridges according to the directions for boning chicken. Then cut them in halves. Cut one dozen mushrooms or truffles into thin slices. Cut one pound of ham into dice. Cut six hard-boiled eggs into slices. Chop some parsley very fine. Have ready one batch of puff paste and half the quantity of suet paste. Roll half the puff paste down to the thickness of one-third of an inch. Grease a French pie-mould and line it carefully with this sheet of paste. With a sharp knife cut the paste even with the top of the mould. Roll the suet paste down to the thickness of a quarter of an inch, and cut it into pieces one inch square. Now put a layer of birds in the bottom of mould, then a sprinkling of ham, salt, pepper, parsley, hard-boiled eggs, and squares of the suet paste, a few bits of butter here and there; now another layer of birds, and so on until all the materials are used. Now roll out for the top crust the remainder of the puff paste, wet the edges of the under-crust with cold water, put the paste for the cover in the pie, and press it gently with the thumb to cement the two edges together, with a sharp knife cut off the upper paste even with the mould. Make a hole in the middle of the top crust. Roll out these trimmings of the paste and cut into leaf-shaped pieces, form and pinch them together in the shape of a flower and place in the hole of the upper crust. Brush the cover of the pie with beaten egg, and bake in a moderately quick oven (about 400° Fahr.) for two hours. While the pie is baking, take the bones, hearts and livers of the birds, put them in a saucepan and cover with a quart of cold water; add a slice of onion and a bay leaf and simmer gently until the pie is done; then strain. Put two tablespoonfuls of butter in a frying pan and stir until a dark brown; then add two tablespoonfuls of flour; mix until smooth; add one pint of the stock from bones and livers, and stir constantly until it boils; add six mushrooms, chopped very fine; season with salt and pepper to taste; take from the fire, add the well-beaten yolks of two eggs, and, if you use wine, one tablespoonful of sherry. Pour the sauce in the pie through a funnel placed in the hole on the top, being careful not to break the flower. Lift the pie carefully on to a heated dish, remove the mould, and serve.

Or, omit the sauce and allow the pie to cool. When cold, garnish with aspic jelly cut into fancy shapes, and put on the dish and around the top of the pie.

Fricassee of Rabbit

Skin and singe the rabbit; remove the intestines. Wash the rabbit quickly and wipe it dry; it is far better to wipe it, inside and out, with a damp cloth, without putting it in water. Split the rabbit down the back; cut each half into four pieces. Put a quarter of a pound of bacon into a saucepan and try out all the fat. Roll the rabbit in flour, drop it into the hot fat and turn until it is nicely browned; then draw it to one side of the saucepan and add two tablespoonfuls of Robin Hood flour to the fat, mix, and add a pint of stock or water, a teaspoonful of salt and a saltspoonful of pepper. Cover and simmer gently until the rabbit is tender, or put it at once into the fireless cooker for four hours.

Serve with rice or potato croquettes.

This recipe will answer also for fricassee of chicken.

Nut Stuffing

Two cupfuls of mashed potatoes, hot.
Half cupful of English walnut or pecan meats.
One tablespoonful of butter.
Four tablespoonfuls of milk or cream.
One tablespoonful of chopped parsley.
One teaspoonful of salt.
A saltspoonful of black pepper.

Put the nuts through the meat grinder, add them to the hot potatoes and add all the other ingredients; stir for a minute over the fire, and use it at once for tame ducks.

The Merry Friar
carrieth Robin

Meat & Fish Sauces

Fish and Meat Sauces and Gravies

There is a philosophy in the making of sauces which, if understood, enables the ordinary cook to make from one rule a dozen different sauces. For instance, two level tablespoonfuls of butter or fat mixed with two level tablespoonfuls of flour are sufficient to thicken a half pint of liquid. This liquid may be water, or milk, strained tomato, stock; or half stock and half milk; or half stock and half strained tomato. Each of these liquids, with appropriate seasonings, gives the name to the sauce.

For all sauces first blend the fat and the flour; add the liquid, stir continually until it reaches the boiling point, seasoning lightly and harmoniously, and strain. Stock makes a better sauce than water for meats and game.

Sauce Bechamel

Two tablespoonfuls of butter.
Two tablespoonfuls of Robin Hood flour.
Half cupful of stock.
Half cupful of milk.
Half teaspoonful of salt.
A dash of pepper.
The yolk of one egg.

Rub the butter and flour together, fill the cup half full of stock, and then to the top with milk, add this, stir until boiling, add the seasoning, take from the fire and add the yolk, beaten. Do not boil a second time; the egg will curdle.

Brown Sauce

Two tablespoonfuls of butter.
Two tablespoonfuls of Robin Hood flour.
Half pint of stock.
Half teaspoonful of salt.
Half saltspoonful of pepper.
Half teaspoonful of onion juice.
One teaspoonful of kitchen bouquet or browning.

Melt the butter and stir it until it begins to turn brown; be careful it does not burn or it will spoil the sauce; add the flour, mix well, add the stock, stir continually until it boils, add the kitchen bouquet or browning, onion juice, salt and pepper, and let this simmer gently for about two minutes, and it is ready for use.

This may be made into mushroom sauce by cooking the mushrooms in the stock and adding them with the stock.

Bread Sauce for Game

One pint of milk.
Half pint of soft bread crumbs.
Half saltspoonful of ground mace.
A tablespoonful of onion juice.
Two tablespoonfuls of butter.
One bay leaf.
Half teaspoonful of salt.
A saltspoonful of pepper.

Put the milk in a double boiler, add the onion, mace and bread; stir and cook five minutes, press through a sieve, return to the fire, add the butter, salt and pepper; as soon as the butter is melted, pour the sauce in a sauce boat and send to the table.

Cream Sauce

Two tablespoonfuls of butter.
Two tablespoonfuls of Robin Hood flour.
Half pint of milk.
Half teaspoonful of salt.
A dash of pepper.

Rub the butter and flour together, add the milk, stir until boiling, add the salt and pepper and it is ready to use.

An Egg Sauce

Add two hard boiled eggs, chopped fine, to the cream sauce after it is taken from the fire.

Onion Sauce

Add two mashed boiled onions to cream sauce after you have taken it from the fire.

Tomato Sauce

Two tablespoonfuls of butter.
Two tablespoonfuls of Robin Hood flour.
One pint of stewed or canned tomatoes.
One bay leaf.
One small onion.
A blade of mace.
Half teaspoonful of salt.
A dash of pepper.

Put the tomatoes over the fire with the onion, bay leaf, mace, salt and pepper; simmer slowly for ten minutes. Melt the butter, add the flour, mix until smooth; add the tomatoes, strained through a sieve. Stir continually until the sauce boils and it is ready for use.

This is usually served with breaded chops, beef croquettes or a panned round steak.

Cream of Tomato Sauce

After you have taken tomato sauce from the fire stir into it three tablespoonfuls of thick cream.

English Drawn Butter

Three tablespoonfuls of butter.
Two tablespoonfuls of Robin Hood flour.
Half pint of water.
Half teaspoonful of salt.
A dash of Tobasco.

Rub two tablespoonfuls of the butter and the flour together, add the water slowly, boiling hot; when this is smooth and thick bring it to a boil, take from the fire, add the seasoning and the remaining tablespoonful of butter, cut into bits. Serve with boiled asparagus, fish, boiled cucumber, vegetable marrow, or plain boiled egg plant.

Plain Sauce Hollandaise

Make an English drawn butter according to the preceding recipe, and when you take it from the fire add the yolks of two eggs, slightly beaten, and a tablespoonful of vinegar or the juice of half a lemon.

Caper Sauce

Make an English drawn butter, and stir in two tablespoonfuls of capers.

Mint Sauce

One bunch (ten stalks) of mint.
Four tablespoonfuls of vinegar.
Two tablespoonfuls of granulated or brown sugar.
Half teaspoonful of salt.
A dash of pepper.

Wash the mint, strip the leaves from the stalks and chop them fine; put them in a bowl or mortar with the sugar and pound until the leaves are reduced to a pulp. Add the salt and pepper, turn into a sauce boat and add the vinegar, little by little. Serve with lamb or mutton.

Gravy

The difference between a gravy and a sauce is that one is made in the pan in which meat or fowls have been roasted. Pour all the fat from the pan except two tablespoonfuls, reserving the brown sediment in the bottom of the pan. Add to the pan two tablespoonfuls of Robin Hood flour, mix thoroughly and add a half pint of stock or water, a half teaspoonful of salt and a dash of pepper. Stir until the sauce boils and is smooth, then add a teaspoonful of browning or kitchen bouquet and strain the gravy into the gravy boat.

This rule will answer for chicken, turkey, beef, mutton or pork.

Forcemeats and Stuffings

Forcemeats are made as a rule into small balls, used as a garnish to meats and soups. Ham forcemeat is frequently used for stuffing turkey or chicken, especially boned turkey; calves' head forcemeat balls are heated in calves' head soup. One recipe will answer for many kinds of forcemeats; simply substitute one meat for another.

Ham Forcemeat

One pint of cold cooked ham, chopped fine.
Half pint of dry bread crumbs.
One pint of milk.
Yolks of three eggs.
One teaspoonful of French mustard.
One tablespoonful of chopped parsley.
A dash of cayenne.

Boil the bread and milk together for a minute; add hastily the yolks of the eggs, stir a minute over the fire, take from the fire and add all the other ingredients. When cool it is ready for use. This makes a nice stuffing for boned turkey, beef à la mode, game, tame ducks, and may be made into small balls, fried in deep fat and used as a garnish for meat dishes.

"Allan-a-Dale's wooing prospers"

Eggs

To ascertain the freshness of an egg before breaking it, hold it between yourself and the sun or a strong light, or drop it in a bucket of water; in the first instance, if fresh you can see the outline of the yolk; if it falls to the bottom of the bucket of water it is fresh.

To preserve eggs, put them in a cask and cover with salt, or lime water. My experience with lime water has been very good; add eggs from day to day as you gather them and keep up the lime water so every egg is thoroughly covered, always packing them small ends down.

Beauregard Eggs

Five eggs.
Two tablespoonfuls of Robin Hood flour.
Two tablespoonfuls of butter.
Five squares of toast.
Half pint, or one cupful of milk.
Half teaspoonful of salt.
A saltspoonful of pepper.

Cover the eggs with warm water, bring quickly to a boil, boil twenty-five minutes and remove the shells; chop the whites fine, or put them through a vegetable press. Rub the yolks through a sieve, keeping them separate. Rub the butter and flour together in a saucepan, add the milk, and when boiling add the whites, salt and pepper. Toast the bread, put it over the bottom of a hot platter, pour over the white sauce, cap the top thoroughly and lightly with the yolks of the eggs, put over a little salt and send at once to the table.

Eggs Benedict

Pull apart, without cutting, English muffins or ordinary light biscuits made with yeast, toast them carefully, put them on a platter, put on each a square of broiled ham, on top of this a poached egg, cover the whole neatly with sauce Hollandaise, dust on top a little chopped truffle, chopped parsley or chopped mushrooms.

Deviled Eggs

Hard boil a dozen eggs, remove the shells, cut the eggs into halves crosswise and take out the yolks without breaking the whites. Press the yolks through a sieve, and add four tablespoonfuls of finely chopped cooked chicken, ham or tongue; add a saltspoonful of salt, a dash of pepper and two tablespoonfuls of cream or olive oil, or melted butter. Rub the mixture to a paste, form into balls the size of the yolks, put them back into the places from which they were taken, put the halves together and roll them quickly in fringed wax or tissue paper, giving the ends a twist like the ordinary secrets.

These are exceedingly nice for cold collations, alfresco meals or picnics.

Eggs Jefferson

Select good sized solid tomatoes, one for each person; cut a slice from the blossom end, scoop out the seeds and core; stand the tomatoes in a baking pan and put in each a tiny bit of butter the size of a pea and a dusting of salt and pepper. Run them in the oven until smoking hot; break into each one whole fresh egg and put them back in the oven until the eggs are "set." Have ready a round of toasted bread for each tomato, stand the tomato in the centre of the toast and send at once to the table.

To give variety, the bottom of the dish may be filled with cream sauce and the toast arranged in it, then put a tablespoonful of the cream sauce on the top of each egg.

Eggs à la Martin

Make a cream sauce, put one half of it in the bottom of a shallow baking dish, break into it the desired quantity of eggs (from four to six), cover over the remaining half of the sauce, dust thickly with grated cheese and bake in the oven five to six minutes, until the eggs are "set." Serve in the dish in which they are cooked.

Eggs
Continued

Eggs à la Tripe

Hard boil six eggs; remove the shells and cut the eggs crosswise into rather thick slices. Slice three Bermuda or one small Spanish onion, or three white-skinned onions, into rings; cover with boiling water, boil rapidly ten minutes, drain, cover again with fresh water and boil until tender, about twenty minutes; drain, this time saving the water. Put two tablespoonfuls of butter and two of Robin Hood flour in a saucepan, mix, and add a half pint of the water in which the onions were boiled, stir until boiling, add a half teaspoonful of salt, a saltspoonful of black pepper, the juice of half a lemon, a grating of nutmeg and two tablespoonfuls of thick cream; when this is hot add the eggs and onions carefully; toss with a fork without breaking either. When thoroughly hot, dish them in a conical form on a small platter, garnish with triangular pieces of toast and serve at once.

Plain Omelet

Put a tablespoonful of butter in a shallow frying pan and melt carefully. Beat four eggs lightly without separating, add four tablespoonfuls of cold water and a dash of pepper; when the butter is very hot, pour in the omelet, dust it quickly with a half teaspoonful of salt, shake, with a limber knife lift the edges, allowing the soft portion to run underneath. When the omelet is "set," fold it over and turn it on to a heated dish.

A plain omelet may be garnished with carefully cooked peas, or tomato sauce, or creamed asparagus tips, or creamed oysters.

A plain omelet is used generally for breakfast, the garnished omelets for luncheon or supper.

English Omelet

Separate six eggs. Have ready a half cupful of cooked meat, chopped fine. Beat the whites of the eggs until they are very stiff; beat the yolks and add them to the whites; add a half teaspoonful of salt and a dash of pepper. Heat a large shallow pan, cover the bottom thoroughly with melted butter or olive oil, turn in the eggs, brown quickly on top of the stove and stand the pan in a hot oven until the omelet is "set." Heat the meat over hot water, put it in the centre, roll the omelet and send it to the table.

Scrambled Eggs

Break six eggs in a bowl and beat them gently until all the yolks are broken. Put a piece of butter the size of a walnut in a frying pan and put over the fire to melt; as soon as it is hot, turn in the eggs and stir continually until they are set. Serve immediately.

Shirred Eggs

Put a bit of butter the size of a pea into the bottom of individual ramekin dishes, break on top a fresh egg, stand these in a pan of water in the oven until the eggs are "set," dust with salt and pepper and send to the table.

Eggs à la Bechamel

Six eggs.
One tablespoonful of Robin Hood flour.
One gill of cream.
One tablespoonful of butter.
One gill of white or veal stock.
Yolk of one egg.
Salt and pepper to taste.

Boil the eggs fifteen minutes; while they are boiling, prepare the sauce as follows: Melt the butter in a frying pan, being careful not to brown it; add to it the flour, mix until smooth; add the stock and cream, and stir continually until it boils; add salt and pepper and stand it over the tea kettle to keep warm while you shell the eggs. Cut the whites into thin shreds, chop the yolks into tiny squares, then pile them in the centre of a shallow, heated dish, and arrange the whites around them. Give the sauce a stir and pour it around the eggs.

Eggs for Breakfast

Six eggs.
One tablespoonful of Robin Hood flour.
One slice of onion.
Six mushrooms.
One tablespoonful of butter.
Two tablespoonfuls of cream.
One bay leaf.
One-half pint of white stock.

Boil the eggs for fifteen minutes. Remove the shells, take out the yolks, being careful not to break them; cut the whites and the mushrooms into dice. Put the butter on to melt, add the flour, mix until smooth; add the stock and cream, stir continually until it boils; add the salt and pepper, the whites of the eggs, and the mushrooms, stir over the fire until it comes again to a boil, throw in the yolks and let it stand over the tea kettle for one or two minutes until the yolks are heated. Serve in a small shallow dish.

"Robin Hood slayeth Guy of Gisborne"

Vegetables

Vegetables

Green vegetables should be freshly gathered, washed in cold water, soaked until crisp and put over the fire in freshly-boiled water. Top-ground vegetables should have salt added to the water; underground vegetables are better cooked without salt. At high altitude many vegetables cook better in a fireless cooker. All dry, leguminous seeds, as old peas, beans and lentils, cannot be made palatable at high altitude unless they are cooked in a fireless cooker.

Boiled Asparagus

Wash, trim and tie the asparagus into bunches. Keep it in cold water until cooking time. Drain and cover with boiling water, boil twenty minutes, add a teaspoonful of salt and boil twenty minutes longer; at high altitude boil ten minutes and put in a fireless cooker for two hours. Serve on squares of toasted bread, garnished with cream sauce.

Or, serve plain with sauce Hollandaise.

Lima Beans

Shell, cover with freshly boiled soft water, boil at sea level thirty minutes, at high altitude one hour, or cook two hours in a fireless cooker. At serving time drain, add butter, salt and pepper, or add salt, pepper and a half cupful of cream.

A sprig of mint boiled with the beans is a great improvement.

Dry Lima Beans

Wash and soak the beans over night in cold water; in the morning drain off the water, cover with fresh cold water, bring to boiling point, boil fifteen minutes, drain again and throw away the water. Cover with fresh boiling water, boil fifteen minutes in high altitude and put into a fireless cooker over night; at sea level they may be simmered gently for two hours. At serving time drain, add salt, pepper and butter, or cream.

This recipe will answer for all kinds of dry beans. Dried beans when cooked may be pressed through a sieve, milk added to the pulp, the whole turned into a baking dish and baked in a quick oven for one hour.

String Beans

Break the blossom end of the bean, and pull it back, removing the strings; pare a thin strip from the other edge of the pod, cut the beans into small pieces crosswise, or three lengthwise; soak in cold water for an hour if possible, then cover with boiling water, boil slowly one hour, drain and add cream, salt and pepper, or butter, salt and pepper.

Frijoles

Soak a half pint of red kidney beans over night in cold water; next morning drain, cover with cold water, bring to boiling point and drain again. Cover with boiling water and cook slowly for two hours at sea level; at high altitude it is best to put them in a fireless cooker over night. At serving time put into a shallow pan two tablespoonfuls of butter or olive oil, when hot add two tablespoonfuls of flour, mix, add six sweet Spanish peppers that have been chopped fine, cooked and pressed through a sieve; or you may use the canned pimentos. Add a half cupful of stock, when boiling add a teaspoonful of salt and two tablespoonfuls of tomato catsup; add the beans, cover the saucepan and stew slowly thirty minutes. The beans must be perfectly tender, but whole.

This is one of the nicest of the bean dishes.

Vegetables
Continued

Stewed Beets

Wash the beets carefully without breaking the skin, cover them with boiling water and cook for one or one and a half hours, until tender. When done throw them in a pan of cold water; rub off the skins and cut the beets into dice. Put two tablespoonfuls of butter and two of flour in a saucepan, mix, and add a half pint of water, stir until boiling, add a half teaspoonful of salt, a saltspoonful of pepper and the beets. Cover and let these reheat for at least twenty minutes, then add two tablespoonfuls of cream and they are ready for use.

Cold plain boiled beets left over may be covered with vinegar and used as a garnish for salads.

Cabbage and Corned Beef

Wash four pounds of corned brisket, put it in a large kettle, cover with cold water, bring to boiling point and simmer two hours. In the meantime remove the outside leaves from a good sized, hard head of cabbage, cut it into quarters, soak it in cold water, add it to the meat at the end of the two hours, and simmer one hour longer. At high altitude this may be cooked over night in a fireless cooker. Serve the cabbage in the centre of the plate, the meat sliced and put around the edge. Pass with it tomato catsup, mustard and horse-radish.

Stewed Cabbage

Chop fine sufficient cabbage for the quantity desired, soak it in cold water one hour, drain, put it into a kettle of boiling water, and at high altitude boil three-quarters of an hour. Be careful the cabbage does not lose its color. At sea level twenty to thirty minutes will be long enough. When tender, drain, return it to the kettle, add two level tablespoonfuls of butter rubbed with two level tablespoonfuls of flour; when this is melted over the cabbage add a half cupful of milk, a half teaspoonful of salt and a saltspoonful of pepper; bring to boiling point, and stand it over a moderate fire for five or ten minutes until the cabbage seems to absorb the sauce.

This is one of the nicest of all the cabbage dishes.

Boiled Cauliflower

Wash and trim the cauliflower, soak it in cold water for an hour, tie it in a piece of cheese cloth, drop it in a kettle of rapidly boiling water, stem downwards; add a teaspoonful of salt and boil thirty minutes at sea level, forty-five minutes at high altitude. It must not lose its color. When done lift carefully from the water, untie the cloth, stand it in a round shallow dish, stem downwards, pour over cream sauce, dust with chopped parsley and serve.

Left-over cauliflower may be chopped, put into a shallow baking dish, covered with cream sauce, dusted with bread crumbs and a little grated cheese, and browned in the oven.

Brussels Sprouts

Wash and trim the sprouts; keep them in cold water until crisp. Drain, cover with boiling water, add a quarter of a teaspoonful of bi-carbonate of soda, boil rapidly in an uncovered saucepan for twenty minutes, then drain and serve with melted butter or cream sauce.

Corn Pudding

One dozen large ears of corn.
Four eggs.
One pint of milk.
One teaspoonful of salt.
Quarter teaspoonful of black pepper.

Score the corn down the centre of each row of corn, and with a dull knife press out the pulp. Separate the eggs, beat the yolks, add them to the corn, mix thoroughly, then add the salt, pepper and milk. Fold in carefully the well-beaten whites of the eggs and bake in a slow oven one hour. Serve cut into squares, as a garnish to roasted beef or lamb, or with creamed chipped beef.

Corn Oysters

Score and press out the corn from one dozen ears. Beat two eggs separately, add the yolks to the corn, mix and add a half teaspoonful of salt, a saltspoonful of pepper, four level tablespoonfuls of Robin Hood flour and then the whites of the eggs. Cook by dropping spoonfuls into hot, shallow fat. When brown on one side, turn and brown on the other, drain and serve.

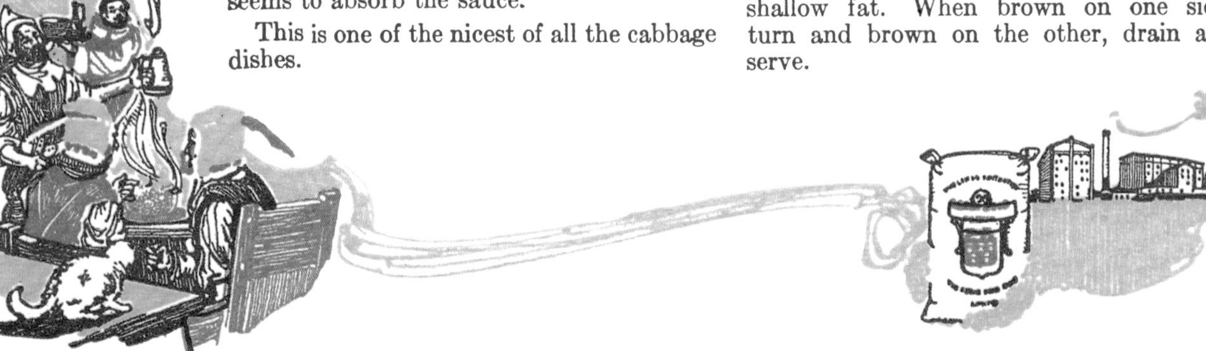

Stewed Cucumbers

A good sized solid cucumber, when well cooked, tastes much like vegetable marrow. Pare, cut into halves, scoop out the seeds, and cut each half in two crosswise. Soak until crisp, throw them into boiling salted water, cook slowly for a half hour, drain, dish and cover with cream sauce.

Boiled Dandelions

Wash and trim very young dandelions, throw them into a hot kettle with very little water, add a teaspoonful of salt, cover and cook slowly one hour, using as little water as possible. Twenty minutes before the dandelions are done add one pound of sliced bacon. At serving time, heap the dandelions in the centre of a large platter, cover over the bacon and send to the table.

Many persons prefer the bacon broiled and used as a garnish.

This recipe will also answer for kale, savoy or spinach.

Fried Egg Plant

Cut a good sized egg plant into thin slices, pare, sprinkle each slice with salt and pepper, dip quickly in an egg beaten with a tablespoonful of water, roll in bread crumbs and fry in a small quantity of very hot fat. When the egg plant is crisp, drain and send to the table with either Chili sauce or tomato catsup.

Egg Plant, West Indian Style

Cut medium sized egg plant into slices a half inch thick, pare, cut each slice into blocks, put them in a kettle with two good sized onions, sliced, a level teaspoonful of salt, a saltspoonful of pepper; add a half cupful of water, cover and stew for thirty minutes, until the egg plant is tender. Take from the fire, add either one cupful of cold oatmeal porridge or farina porridge, or stale bread crumbs; two tablespoonfuls of butter and a dash of Tobasco; mix with a silver fork. Put the mixture in a baking dish, cover the top with squares of buttered bread and bake in a moderate oven a half hour.

Stewed Carrots

If the carrots are young they may simply be cooked whole; it will require about one hour to make them tender; they may then be served with melted butter or with cream sauce.

Breakfast Cereal or Farina Croquettes

Add a half cupful of Robin Hood Breakfast Cereal to one pint of milk and stand in a cold place over night. In the morning put in a double boiler, cook until you have a thick, smooth mass, add the yolks of three eggs, take from the fire, add a level teaspoonful of salt, a saltspoonful of pepper, a grating of nutmeg, a teaspoonful of onion juice and a tablespoonful of chopped parsley. Mix and form into cylinders two inches long; dip in egg beaten with a tablespoonful of water, roll in bread crumbs and fry in deep hot fat. Serve as an accompaniment to roasted duck or goose. With cream sauce these make a very nice dish for supper or luncheon.

Stewed Mushrooms

Wash the mushrooms, remove the stems, cut them into slices and put them in a porcelain or granite kettle. To each pound add a half cupful of milk, two tablespoonfuls of butter, a half teaspoonful of salt and a saltspoonful of pepper. Cover the kettle and simmer gently for a half hour, then add a half tablespoonful of cornstarch mixed in a little cold milk; bring to a boil and serve on toast.

Mushrooms may be put into a baking pan, skin side down, dusted with salt and pepper. Pat a tiny bit of butter in each, and bake in a quick oven twenty minutes; serve on toast.

Baked Onions

Select large, perfect onions, trim the bottoms but do not peel them. Throw them into boiling water, add a teaspoonful of salt and boil rapidly twenty minutes. Drain in a colander, dry each carefully in a soft cloth, put it in the centre of a square of waxed paper and twist it at the top. Bake in a slow oven one hour. When done remove the papers, peel the onions, put them in a vegetable dish, dust with salt, pour over melted butter.

Spanish and Bermuda onions are particularly nice cooked in this way.

Vegetables *Continued*

Cymlin

Pare two good sized cymlins, cut them into eighths, cut out the seeds and cook according to the preceding recipe for cucumbers.

Cymlins are very nice served with sauce Hollandaise.

Parsnip Fritters

Scrape and boil four good sized parsnips. When done press through a colander, add a half teaspoonful of salt, two level tablespoonfuls of Robin Hood flour and one egg, well beaten. Form into small cakes and fry in a hot dripping in a shallow pan; brown one side, then turn and brown the other.

Serve with boiled salt fish.

Potatoes au Gratin

Chop cold boiled potatoes rather fine. Make a cream sauce, add the potatoes, turn into a shallow baking dish, dust them thickly with grated cheese, then with bread crumbs, and brown in a quick oven.

Potatoes O'Brien

Cut cold boiled potatoes into dice. Cut an onion into slices a quarter of an inch thick, and cut each slicc into bits the size of the potatoes. Remove the seeds from one green and one red pepper, and cut the flesh the same as the potatoes. Put two tablespoonfuls of dripping or butter in a large shallow frying pan; when hot put in all the ingredients, shake carefully and stir without breaking the potatoes, until nicely browned. Serve on a hot dish dusted with chopped parsley.

Potato Croquettes

Add to one quart of mashed potatoes the yolks of two eggs, a tablespoonful of chopped parsley, a teaspoonful of grated onion, a teaspoonful of salt, a saltspoonful of pepper and two saltspoonfuls of grated nutmeg. Mix, form into cylinders, dip in egg beaten with a tablespoonful of water, roll in bread crumbs and fry in deep hot fat. If the fat is not sufficiently hot, the croquettes will swell and crack. They must brown immediately, and by that time they will be heated through.

Sweet potato croquettes are made in the same way, omitting the onion and nutmeg.

French Fried Potatoes

Pare good sized potatoes, cut them into the desired shape, put them on a towel and sort of pat them until they are dry. Have ready a pan of cool, deep fat (it should register by chemical thermometer 230° to 240° Fahr.). Put in the potatoes and let them sort of stew until the edges begin to turn brown, then lift and throw them in a pan lined with soft paper. This may be done long before the potatoes are needed. At serving time heat the same deep fat, making it quite hot, about 365° Fahr., put a few potatoes at a time in the frying basket, plunge it down in the hot fat, and as soon as the potatoes brown lift them, dust with salt, throw them on a soft paper, and they are ready to serve.

The second cooking makes the potatoes brown and dry and mealy. Potatoes that are cooked from beginning to end in the first fat are not so good. This is also true of Saratoga chips. Slice them thin, cook a few at a time in the fat that is not overheated; after they are drained throw them into very hot fat until crisp, brown and dry.

Hashed Brown Potatoes

Chop cold boiled potatoes, season with salt and pepper. Put two levcl tablespoonfuls of butter or dripping in a shallow frying pan, when hot put in enough potatoes to make a layer of one inch; press them down with a knife and cook slowly fifteen minutes without stirring. Fold one half over the other, turn on to a heated dish.

Spinach, French Fashion

Wash the spinach thoroughly to free it from grit. Pick it from the pan and throw it in another pan; do not drain the water off or the grit will remain. Have ready a kettle, the bottom of which is covered with boiling water, throw in the spinach, dust with salt, cover the kettle and allow it to boil for thirty minutes, then drain in a colander. Chop it fine, put it in a saucepan. and add to each half peck two tablespoonfuls of butter or cream, a level teaspoonful of salt and a saltspoonful of pepper. Stir until thoroughly hot, and serve in a heated dish garnished with small squares of toasted bread and hard boiled eggs.

Baked Pumpkin

Cut a small pumpkin into strips four inches wide, cut these strips into halves, remove the seeds, stand them in a baking pan, dust with salt and pepper, and bake in a moderately quick oven one hour. Serve in the shell.

Curried Tomatoes

Six solid tomatoes.
One good sized onion.
Two teaspoonfuls of curry.
Juice of half a lemon.
Half teaspoonful of salt.

Peel the tomatoes, cut them into halves and squeeze out the seeds. Put two tablespoonfuls of butter into a saucepan, add the onion chopped, shake until the onion is soft, not brown; add the curry powder and a half pint of boiling water. Put in the tomatoes, dust with salt, cover the saucepan and cook slowly ten minutes, add the lemon juice, and they are ready to use. Pass with them a dish of nicely boiled rice. To be absolutely correct, the rice should be put around the edge of the platter, the tomatoes put in the centre, and the whole covered with nicely baked bananas, and the rice garnished here and there with teaspoonfuls of chutney.

Spaghetti, Italian Fashion

Four ounces of spaghetti.
One pint of strained stewed tomatoes.
One onion.
Half pound of lean beef.
Two tablespoonfuls of oil, butter or suet.
Half teaspoonful of salt.
One cupful of grated cheese.
Half cupful of cream.

Put the spaghetti, without breaking, into a large kettle of boiling water, add a teaspoonful of salt and boil rapidly three-quarters of an hour, or put it in a fireless cooker for two hours. Put the butter or oil in a saucepan, add the onion, chopped; shake until the onion is soft, not brown; add the beef, cut into dice, shake until the beef is thoroughly cooked on the outside; add the tomato and salt. Simmer gently for one hour, then drain the spaghetti, dash over some cold water, drain again and put it into the tomato mixture; when thoroughly hot, add the cheese and cream, stir until the cheese is melted, without breaking the spaghetti, and serve.

Another nice way is to reheat the spaghetti in a little stock, seasoning it with salt and pepper, turn it on to a large platter, put over the top the tomato mixture, and pass with it grated Parmesan. This is the true Naples fashion.

Baked Macaroni

Four ounces of macaroni.
Two tablespoonfuls of butter.
Two tablespoonfuls of Robin Hood flour.
Half pint of milk.
One teaspoonful of salt.
A dash of pepper.
Quarter pound of cheese.

Break the macaroni into boiling water, boil three-quarters of an hour, or cook in a fireless cooker two hours; drain. Rub the butter and flour together, add the milk, salt and pepper, and the cheese, grated. Take from the fire, put the macaroni in a baking dish, pour over the cream sauce and cheese, dust the top thickly with bread crumbs and bake in a moderate oven about twenty minutes, or until it is nicely browned.

Asparagus in Ambush

One quart of asparagus tips.
Nine stale breakfast rolls.
One pint of milk.
Four eggs.
One large tablespoonful of butter.
Salt and black pepper to taste.

Wash the asparagus tips, boil fifteen minutes, and drain them in a colander. Cut the tops off the rolls, and take out the crumb, then set them open in the oven to dry, laying each top by the roll from which it was taken. Put the milk on to boil in a farina boiler. Beat the eggs until light, then stir them in the boiling milk, and stir until it begins to thicken; add the butter, salt, and pepper, and take from the fire. Chop the asparagus tips, then add them to the milk. Take the rolls from the oven, fill them with this mixture, put on the tips, and serve hot. Good.

Fried Sweet Potatoes

Skin and cut lengthwise boiled sweet potatoes. Put three tablespoonfuls of dripping in a large frying-pan, dust the potatoes with salt and pepper, throw them into the hot fat, brown first on one side, then turn and brown the other. Serve very hot.

Sauerkraut

Shred the cabbage fine. Line the bottom and sides of a small keg with the green cabbage leaves, put in a layer of the cabbage about three inches thick, cover with four ounces of salt and pound down well, then another layer of cabbage and salt, and so on until the keg is full. Put a board on top of the cabbage, and on this a heavy weight, and stand in a moderately warm place to ferment. The cabbage sinks when the fermentation begins, and the liquor rises to the surface over the cover. Skim off the skum and stand the keg in a cool, dry cellar, and it is ready for use. Cover it closely each time any is taken out. When you use it, wash it in warm water, and boil it with corned beef or salt pork the same as cabbage.

Puree of Peas

One quart of green peas or two pint cans.
One tablespoonful of butter.
One bay leaf.
Two cloves.
One pint of milk.
One pint of water.
One tablespoonful of Robin Hood flour.
One onion.
One sprig of parsley.
Salt and pepper to taste.

Wash the peas in cold water; then put them in a saucepan with the water and boil twenty minutes. When done they should be almost dry. Press through a colander. Put the milk on to boil in a farina boiler. Add the bay leaf, onion, cloves and parsley. Rub the butter and flour together until smooth. Strain the milk into the peas, then return to the farina boiler, stir in the butter and flour, and stir continually until it boils and thickens; then add the salt and pepper, and serve.

Puree of lima, or any other green bean, may be made according to this recipe.

Baked Pumpkin

Cut the pumpkin first in halves, then in quarters; remove the seeds, but not the rind. Place in a baking-pan with the rind downwards, and bake in a slow oven until tender when you pierce with a fork. When done, serve in the rind; help it out by spoonfuls as you would mashed potatoes.

Saratoga Chips

Pare one large potato, and cut in very thin slices, on a vegetable cutter, over a bowl of cold water, so that each slice will fall into the water (this makes them light and dry after being fried); soak ten minutes, take out a few pieces at a time, and dry them on a soft towel. Have ready a kettle of boiling lard. Throw in the slices, a few at a time, stir them with a skimmer; when a light brown, take them out, and place on a piece of soft brown paper in a colander, dredge with salt, and stand in the open oven to keep warm while you fry the remainder. Turn the first from the colander into a hot dish, and skim out the second frying on the paper, and so continue until you have finished.

Spinach

Wash a half-peck of spinach through several waters to free it from grit. Pick it over very carefully and cut off the roots. Wash again, drain, and take up by handfuls, shake and press out all the remaining water. Put it in a kettle,and add one cup of water; cover the kettle, place over a moderate fire, and allow the spinach to thus steam for twenty minutes. Then drain in a colander; turn into a chopping-tray and chop very fine; it cannot be too fine; put into a saucepan with a tablespoonful of butter, salt and pepper to taste, stir until very hot. Have a heated dish at hand, and arrange on it small squares of buttered toast. Mould the spinach by packing it tightly in a cup, and turn each cupful out on a slice of toast. Place half of a hard-boiled egg on the top of each mould. Pour drawn butter around the toast, and serve.

Or, when done, drain, chop fine, serve in a heated vegetable dish. Cut hard-boiled eggs in slices and lay on top.

A half-peck of spinach will serve five people.

Tomato Farci

Put a layer of tomatoes in the bottom of a baking-dish, then a layer of bread crumbs, then a sprinkling of salt and pepper, then another layer of tomatoes, and so continue until the dish is full, having the last layer crumbs. Put a few bits of butter over the top and bake in a quick oven twenty minutes Serve in the dish in which it was baked.

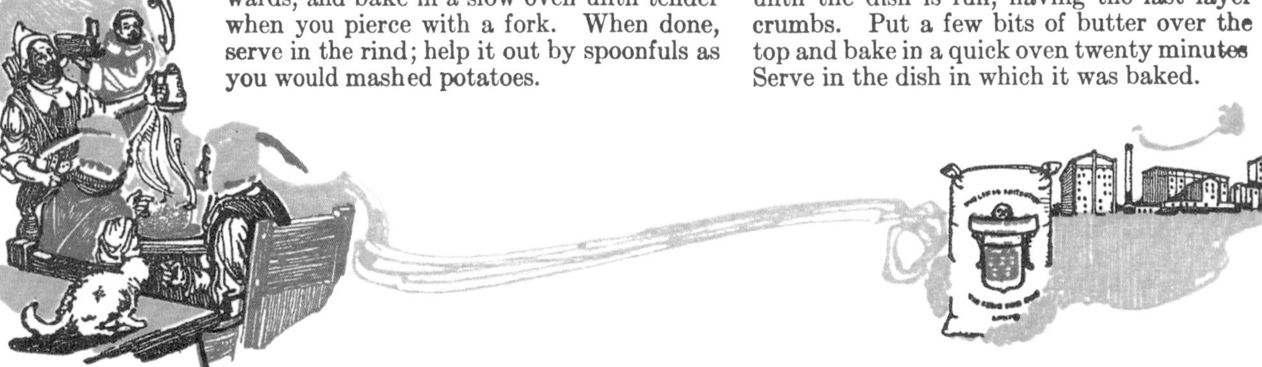

"Maid Marian cometh
to Sherwood Forest"

Salads

Salads

A dinner salad is a dish composed of an uncooked green vegetable, like lettuce, Romaine, chicory or celery, nicely seasoned with salt and pepper, and dressed with a French dressing.

A luncheon or supper salad is composed of a meat and a vegetable material, dressed with a thick mayonnaise dressing.

Spinach, string beans, cauliflower, beets, carrots and potatoes may be cooked, and when cold, used on a bed of lettuce, or alone, as a supper or dinner salad. Raw shaved cabbage, soaked an hour in cold water, is exceedingly good with French dressing. These salads usually accompany meat, while the mayonnaise salads are served in the place of meat.

Nut Dressing

Half tumbler of peanut butter.
Half cupful of water.
Three eggs.
The juice of three lemons.
Half teaspoonful of salt.
A dash of cayenne.

Mix the nut butter and water, add the eggs (well beaten), salt, cayenne and lemon juice; stand the bowl in a saucepan of hot water, beat until the dressing is as thick as mayonnaise, and stand aside to cool. Use with tomatoes, celery, lettuce, chopped beets and potatoes, or peeled tomatoes.

Cooked Salad Dressing

Put a half pint of milk over the fire in double boiler. Moisten two level tablespoonfuls of cornstarch in cold milk, add to the hot milk, stir and cook until thick and smooth, add hastily the beaten yolks of three eggs, take from the fire and when cool add two tablespoonfuls of butter, a half teaspoonful of salt, a dash of cayenne and two tablespoonfuls of vinegar; the whites will be used for another dish.

French Dressing

Half teaspoonful of salt.
Half saltspoonful of pepper.
Two tablespoonfuls of vinegar.
Six tablespoonfuls of olive oil.
A piece of ice the size of an egg.

Put the salt and pepper in a bowl, add the ice, stir until the salt is melted and dissolved, pour in the oil, stir the ice a minute, remove the ice, add the vinegar and beat until creamy and the thickness of good cream. If ice is not at hand, add a teaspoonful of water to the salt, and when it is melted add the oil, mix and add the vinegar. Use at once.

Italian dressing—Add a teaspoonful of tomato catsup to ordinary French dressing.

Ceylon salad dressing—Add a half saltspoonful of curry and a dash of Tobasco to ordinary French dressing.

Mayonnaise Dressing

Put the yolks of three eggs into a clean, cold bowl or soup dish, stand this in cold water or a pan of cracked ice; stir lightly and add, drop by drop, a half pint of cold olive oil; add a teaspoonful of vinegar or lemon juice, a half saltspoonful of salt and a dash of cayenne, and the dressing is ready for use; it may be covered and kept in the refrigerator for several hours.

Where a large quantity of dressing is needed and the cost of oil is an object, add to the mayonnaise just before mixing the salad, a half pint of cream whipped to a stiff froth.

CAUTION: If the oil is added too fast the dressing will separate and become thin. If this occurs, put a hard boiled yolk through a sieve into another dish; when very cold add the spoiled dressing to the hard boiled yolk, a teaspoonful at a time, stirring rapidly all the while.

Do not season the mayonnaise too highly; season the salad materials.

Salads Continued

Chicken Salad

Allow one four-pound chicken, using all the meat except the legs, and four heads of celery, to each eight people; if you serve this on lettuce it will easily serve ten persons. Boil the chicken until it is very tender, remove the skin, and when very cold cut the meat into dice. Sprinkle the meat with a tablespoonful of vinegar, a dusting of pepper and not more than twenty drops of grated onion or onion juice. Wash the celery and cut it into lengths of a half inch; keep this cold until serving time. Make the mayonnaise, using three eggs and a pint of oil, and if you have it, a half pint of whipped cream. At serving time mix the celery and chicken, one quart of each, season it nicely with salt, add sufficient mayonnaise to cover each piece, mix thoroughly, heap on a platter lined thickly with lettuce leaves, or in a salad bowl, cover over the remaining mayonnaise and send to the table. This may be garnished with sweet red peppers cut into strips, capers, hard boiled eggs or olives, or all.

All meat and fish salads are made after this recipe. This recipe will also answer for lobster, crab or fish salad.

Fruit Salad

Peel two grape fruit and four oranges, removing all the white skin. With a sharp knife take out each carpel and remove the seeds. Add two tart apples, pared and cut into thin slices and then into small squares; and any other fruit you have at hand—bananas, white grapes, or the purple California grapes, cut into halves and the seeds removed. Use French dressing or sugar added and the whole seasoned with sherry or Madeira. This is usually served as a dessert, while a regular salad is served after the meat course.

Potato Salad

Boil four good sized potatoes in their jackets; when done and dry, remove the skins and cut them into thin slices. Make a French dressing and add one onion, thinly sliced. Turn the potatoes into this, toss with a fork (without breaking the slices) and stand aside until cold. When cold, dish and garnish with pickled beets and chopped parsley.

My Lady's Salad

Peel six tomatoes, cut them into halves and carefully remove the seeds and core. Pare and cut a small pineapple into dice, mix it with an equal portion of tender white celery cut into half-inch lengths, season it with salt and pepper, mix with mayonnaise dressing and fill the tomato shells. Chop sweet red pepper rather fine, and chop a small quantity of parsley; put the chopped pepper in the centre of each as a garnish, and dust the edges with the chopped parsley. Serve at once.

Waldorf Salad

Mix an equal quantity of white celery and crisp tart apple cut into dice, season with salt and pepper, squeeze over the juice of a lemon, mix with mayonnaise, dish on lettuce leaves and dust thickly with chopped almonds or English walnuts.

Grape Fruit Salad

Pare the grape fruit and remove the white, bitter skin. With a sharp knife take out the entire flesh of each carpel, without breaking it, and arrange these on lettuce leaves. Make a French dressing, using the juice, drained from the grape fruit, instead of the vinegar.

Cucumber Salad

Pare fresh green cucumbers, cut into ice-cold water to soak for an hour; do not add salt. When crisp and brittle, dish, cover with French dressing and serve immediately; if they stand ten minutes they will become wilted and unpalatable.

Swedish Salad

Grate six young carrots, season lightly with salt, and form the mixture into cones, about a tablespoonful in each. Stand these on lettuce leaves, dust thickly with chopped pecan nuts, pour over French dressing and serve.

String Bean Salad

Serve cold string beans with a French dressing. Dish on lettuce or serve alone.

Asparagus Salad

Dish neatly a bunch of boiled asparagus, pour over French dressing and serve at once.

"The New Robin Hood Breakfast Cereal"
"The Heart of the Wheat"

"So Good You Want It Every Morning"

"Robin Hood seeketh
Queen Eleanor"

Cereal Foods

PORRIDGE AND CEREAL FOODS

Rolled Oats Porridge

Put three half-pints of boiling water into a saucepan, add a level teaspoonful of salt, and sprinkle in a half pint of Robin Hood Porridge Oats.

Caution: The water must be rapidly boiling and the oatmeal must be sprinkled in slowly, without stirring. Boil rapidly about five minutes, stand over hot water, or in hot water and cook for one hour.

My Method: I usually do this at night in the upper part of the double boiler, and let it boil while the supper dishes are being washed; the upper part of the boiler is then lifted and put aside over night. Reheat for breakfast. Do not stir porridge too much; it breaks the grain and makes it pasty rather than jelly-like.

Oatmeal Porridge Number Two

Put a pint and a half of boiling water into the upper part of the double boiler, add a teaspoonful of salt, boil rapidly over the fire, and sprinkle in one and a half cupfuls of Robin Hood Porridge Oats, stir for a moment, cook fifteen minutes, then put the upper part of the boiler down in the lower part into the boiling water, add a half pint of milk and cook a half hour.

Oatmeal Mush

One quart of water.
One and one-half cupfuls of Robin Hood Porridge Oats.
A level teaspoonful of salt.

Put the water in a saucepan over the fire and add the salt; sift in the Robin Hood Porridge Oats slowly, so as not to stop the boiling of the water. Boil rapidly for ten minutes, stand the pan in another of hot water and cook slowly for at least one hour, better two. Stir as lightly as possible, and serve. This should be sufficiently thick to drop, not pour, from a spoon.

Oatmeal Gruel

This is an exceedingly nice food for children or for the aged.

Sprinkle one tablespoonful of Robin Hood Porridge Oats into one quart of boiling water, boil an hour and a half, take from the fire and strain; add four tablespoonfuls of good cream, or a tiny bit of butter and milk, and a grating of nutmeg. Serve warm.

This, after it is strained, may be mixed with milk and given to a child that is still being fed from the bottle.

Invalid Gruel

Four tablespoonfuls of Robin Hood Porridge Oats.
One pint of boiling water.
Half teaspoonful of salt.
One egg.
Two tablespoonfuls of cream.

Sprinkle the Porridge Oats and salt into the boiling water, boil rapidly thirty minutes, strain through a fine sieve, reheat and pour slowly into the egg, well beaten; turn this into the gruel bowl and add the cream. Serve hot, either plain, or with toast.

Coddled Apples with Oatmeal

Core six tart apples, stand them in a baking dish and fill the spaces from which the cores were taken with left-over Robin Hood Oats porridge; sprinkle with four tablespoonfuls of sugar, add a half cupful of water, and bake until the apples are tender. Serve hot, with milk or cream. A nice breakfast dish.

Oatmeal Bouchées

Fill small custard cups with left-over porridge, and stand aside until perfectly cold. At serving time, turn out the moulds, scoop out the centres and fill the spaces with finely chopped sugared peaches or other fruits. Serve plain, or with soft custard or milk.

Cereal Foods
Continued

Oatmeal Shortcake

Pour left-over porridge into a small round mould or a good sized baking powder can and stand aside to cool. At serving time, cut it into slices, arrange the slices neatly in a dessert plate, putting a layer of fruit between each slice of cold porridge; dust the whole with powdered sugar and serve it with cream.

This makes an exceedingly nice supper dessert.

Fried Oatmeal

Make a good porridge, turn it into a small square pan until cold, cut it into slices, dust each slice with salt, pepper and flour, and fry them in a small quantity of hot suet, being careful to turn the slices but once. Serve as you would cornmeal mush.

PORRIDGE WHEAT

ROBIN HOOD PORRIDGE WHEAT is the choicest portion of the wheat berry. It is purified, sterilized Farina, put up in an airtight fibre tube to keep it sanitary and free from vermin. The use of Robin Hood Porridge Wheat absolutely does away with the many losses which invariably occur when Farina is bought in bulk.

Porridge Wheat Porridge

Two cupfuls of boiling water.
Half teaspoonful of salt.
Half cupful of Robin Hood Porridge Wheat.
One cupful of milk.

Add the salt to the boiling water, sprinkle in the farina, stirring all the while; boil rapidly ten minutes, stirring now and then. Put the saucepan in another of boiling water, or in the bottom of the double boiler, add the milk and cook ten minutes longer. Serve hot, with milk or cream.

Porridge Wheat Mush

Put one cupful of milk and one cupful of water in the upper part of the double boiler; when the water underneath is boiling, sprinkle in slowly, stirring all the while, six tablespoonfuls of Robin Hood Porridge Wheat. Stir until you have a thick mush, add a half teaspoonful of salt, cover the vessel and cook twenty minutes. Serve with butter or milk, or cream, same as you would cornmeal mush.

It makes very little difference how long these cereals cook; the danger comes from under rather than over-cooking.

Baked Porridge Wheat

One and one-half pints of milk.
Half cupful of Robin Hood Porridge Wheat.
One cupful of chopped nuts.
Half teaspoonful of salt.

Heat the milk in a double boiler, sprinkle in slowly the Porridge Wheat, cook and stir until the mixture thickens, add the salt and nuts, turn the mixture into a baking dish and bake in a quick oven twenty minutes.

Serve for luncheon or supper, and eat it as you would hot mush, with butter.

Porridge Wheat Jelly

One pint of milk.
Six tablespoonfuls of Robin Hood Porridge Wheat.
Four tablespoonfuls of sugar.
Half teaspoonful of salt.
One teaspoonful of vanilla.

Put the milk in a double boiler, add the Porridge Wheat slowly; stir and cook for at least thirty minutes, until the mixture is thick; add the sugar and seasoning, turn into small moulds and stand away to cool.

Serve with plain or whipped cream.

Porridge Wheat Custard

One quart of milk.
Six tablespoonfuls of Robin Hood Porridge Wheat.
Half cupful of sugar.
Four eggs.
A teaspoonful of vanilla.

Cook the Porridge Wheat in the milk, in a double boiler, for at least thirty minutes—in fact, the farina may be added to the cold milk, soaked for a half hour and then cooked a half hour. Beat the eggs and sugar until light, add them to the hot mixture, stir and cook about three minutes, as you would a soft custard; take from the fire, add the vanilla, turn at once into the serving dish and stand aside to cool. Serve with cream or cream sauce.

This may also be filled into small moulds or cups, and turned out into individual dishes.

Cream Porridge

Put one pint of boiling water in a double boiler, add a half teaspoonful of salt and one cupful of milk; when this is boiling stir in carefully five tablespoonfuls of Robin Hood Porridge Wheat, stir until the mixture thickens, cover and cook twenty minutes.

Left-over cream porridge may be used with fruit, served with plain or whipped cream, as dessert; or it may be moulded in small moulds, dusted with powdered sugar and served with soft custard, or it may be served cold, with plain cream.

Cream porridge with fruit makes an excellent supper dish for children

Robin Hood Spoon Bread

Put a pint of milk in a double boiler. When hot, sprinkle in four tablespoonfuls of Robin Hood Porridge Wheat, stir until you have a smooth, thick mush, add a half teaspoonful of salt, take from the fire, drop in the yolks of four eggs, mix thoroughly, stir in the well-beaten whites of the eggs, turn into a casserole or baking dish and bake in a moderately quick oven three-quarters of an hour. Serve in the dish in which it was baked. Dish with a spoon and eat it as you would hot mush, with butter.

One of the most delightful of the hot breads.

Cracked Wheat

One quart of water.
One teaspoonful of salt.
Six tablespoonfuls of cracked wheat.

Mix the wheat, water and salt together; put this in the farina boiler, and boil four hours, or over night, on the back part of the stove. Serve warm, with sugar and cream.

Rye Mush

One quart of boiling water.
One teaspoonful of salt.
Five heaping tablespoonfuls of rye meal.

Sift the meal into the boiling water, stirring all the while; add the salt, stir until it boils again, cover, and cook slowly one hour. Serve with sugar and cream.

Hulled Corn (Mrs. Adams)

Put two handfuls of clean hard-wood ashes in two quarts of cold water; boil fifteen or twenty minutes; let stand until the ashes settle and the water is perfectly clear. To this cleansed water (it should be strong enough of the lye to feel a little slippery), add as much cold water as is necessary to cover the corn. Put the corn in the water; let it boil until the hulls begin to start, then skim the corn out into a pan of clear, cold water, and rub thoroughly with the hands, to remove the hulls and cleanse the corn from the lye;—rub it through two, three, or even four waters, that there may be no taste of lye; then put into clear water and boil until tender.

Boiled Rice

Wash one cup of rice. Put three quarts of boiling water into a kettle, add a teaspoonful of salt, and let it boil rapidly; sprinkle in the rice so gradually that you will not stop the boiling. When you have it all in, give the water a twirl with a fork, cover the kettle and boil rapidly twenty minutes. Then pour into a colander to drain. Place the colander on a tin dish; stand it in the oven for five minutes to dry, leaving the door wide open; then turn carefully into a heated dish. Serve without a cover.

Points to be remembered:—Boil rapidly from the time you cover the kettle till you take it off. The rapid boiling allows each grain to swell three times its normal size, and the motion prevents the grains from sticking together. Do not stir it, as this will cause it to fall to the bottom of the kettle, and burn. The drying in the oven with the door open evaporates the moisture, leaving the rice soft, snowy white, and perfectly dry.

Boiled Rice (Italian Style)

Wash one cup of rice in cold water, and drain it. Have a three-quart kettle nearly full of boiling water; add to it a slice of bacon, a tablespoonful of grated Parmesan, and a pinch of saffron; add the rice gradually and finish according to the recipe for Boiled Rice.

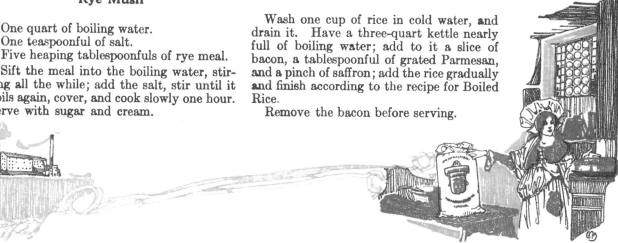

Remove the bacon before serving.

Boiled Barley

Wash the barley through several cold waters, then cover with cold water; bring quickly to a boil; boil five minutes; drain, cover with fresh boiling water, and boil slowly four hours.

To Make a Rice Border

Wash one cup of rice in cold water, and drain it. Put it in a saucepan with one quart of boiling stock. Boil rapidly for fifteen minutes, then stand it over a very moderate fire to steam (not boil) for twenty minutes longer; drain, season with salt and black pepper, and press into a well-buttered border mould. Then put it in the oven and bake fifteen minutes. Take out; place a dish on the mould; turn it upside down, and remove the mould.

The hollow space in the centre may be filled with a white or brown fricassee of chicken or a curry.

Rice Croquettes No. 1

One pint of milk.
Yolks of two eggs.
One-half teaspoonful of vanilla.
One quarter cup of currants.
One-half cup of rice.
Two large tablespoonfuls of sugar.
One-quarter cup of raisins.
One-quarter cup of citron.

Wash the rice and put it in a farina boiler with the milk, and boil until very thick; now add the yolks of the eggs, and the sugar; beat until smooth. Take from the fire, add the vanilla, and the fruit well floured. Turn out on a dish to cool. When cold, form into pyramids; dip first in beaten egg, then in bread crumbs, and fry in boiling oil or fat.

Put a small piece of currant jelly on the top of each croquette; dust the whole with powdered sugar and serve with Vanilla Sauce.

This quantity will make twelve croquettes.

Rice Croquettes No. 2

One quart of milk.
Salt and white pepper to taste.
One cup of rice.
One tablespoonful of chopped parsley.
Yolks of four eggs.

Wash the rice and put it in a farina boiler with the milk; boil about one hour, or until very thick; then beat until smooth; add the yolks of the eggs, and cook ten minutes longer. Take from the fire; add the parsley and seasoning; mix well, turn out on a plate, and stand away until very cold. Then form into cylinders; dip first in beaten egg, then in bread crumbs, and fry in boiling oil or fat.

Baked Macaroni

Quarter pound of macaroni.
Quarter pound of grated cheese.
Half cup of cream.
One tablespoonful of butter.
Salt and pepper.

Break the macaroni in convenient lengths, put it in a two-quart kettle and nearly fill the kettle with boiling water; add a teaspoonful of salt, and boil rapidly twenty-five minutes (the rapid boiling prevents the macaroni from sticking together); drain in a colander; then throw into cold water to blanch for ten minutes; then drain again in the colander. Put a layer of the macaroni in the bottom of a baking dish; then a layer of cheese, then a sprinkling of salt and pepper, then another layer of macaroni, and so continue until all is used, having the last layer macaroni. Cut the butter in small bits; distribute them evenly over the top; add the cream and bake until a golden brown (about twenty minutes) in a moderately quick oven. Serve in the dish in which it was baked.

Macaroni Croquettes

Six ounces of macaroni.
One tablespoonful of butter.
Two tablespoonfuls of grated cheese.
Half pint of milk.
Two tablespoonfuls of Robin Hood flour.
Yolks of three eggs.
Salt and pepper to taste.

Break the macaroni in pieces about two inches long. Put it in a kettle nearly full of boiling water, and boil rapidly twenty-five minutes. When done, put it in a colander to drain, then into cold water for fifteen minutes; drain again, and then cut it in pieces a half-inch long. Put the milk on to boil. Rub the butter and flour together until smooth; stir into the milk when boiling, and stir continually until it thickens; then add the cheese and macaroni, salt, pepper, and the yolks of the eggs; cook one minute longer; then turn out on a plate to cool. When cold, form into cone-shaped croquettes; roll first in egg and then in bread crumbs, and fry in boiling fat. Serve with Cream Sauce.

"The Outlaw shooteth in King Harry's Tourney"

Bread

Home Made Yeast

Grate four good sized potatoes into one quart of boiling water, boil five minutes, stirring constantly; take from the fire and turn into a stone or glass jar. When this is cool add a half cupful of sugar, two tablespoonfuls of salt and a half cupful of yeast or one compressed yeast cake dissolved in a little warm water. Stand a saucer over the top of the jar and put it in a warm place (about 68° Fahr.). Each time the contents come to the top, stir it down, and continue stirring it down until the fermentation stops; this will take perhaps a half day, or more. Then stir the yeast, put it in good sized bottles or jars with screw tops, and put it in a cold place until wanted. This will keep in the winter for two weeks, and in the refrigerator in the summer quite as long. One cupful of this yeast will make four loaves of bread.

Bread

The recipes following are written especially for the Robin Hood flour. This flour, being of the most excellent quality (a strong spring wheat), will require more moisture than most flour purchased in the open market. Even at a high price good flour is cheap. I prefer in giving recipes to give the quantity of liquid, and allow the housekeeper to add flour until she has a dough of the proper consistency. New flour requires less moisture than flour that has been slightly aged, so an exact quantity might make a failure.

The mixing is called "sponging," and in these days, after giving the sponge a thorough beating, we continue adding flour until we have a dough which can be thoroughly kneaded. Each grain of flour must be surrounded by a volume of water to hydrate the starch; this softens the starch, moistens the gluten and dissolves the natural sugar and albumin, which makes a compact fine-grained loaf. The kneading is really the most important part of bread making; this may be done by the hands, or with machines made for the purpose. When the dough becomes elastic and loses its stickiness, it has been kneaded sufficiently long and is ready for its first standing. Milk makes a whiter and finer grained bread than water alone. An exceedingly good liquid is half milk and half water, but the quantities of water alone will be the same.

If too much flour is added the bread will be good the first day, but will dry quickly. Make the dough as soft as you can handle it; the kneading will remove the stickiness.

Ye Perfect Bread

Scald one pint of milk, add one pint of water, a half teaspoonful of salt, and when the mixture is lukewarm add one compressed yeast cake dissolved in a half cupful of warm water, or one cupful of home-made yeast, or two dry cakes. Measure two quarts of Robin Hood flour, and add the flour slowly, beating all the while; when you have a thick dough, remove the spoon, take a knife and cut the flour in, folding the dough over and over with the knife. When sufficiently stiff to knead, take it on the board and knead until it loses its stickiness and the dough is soft and elastic. Beat it for five minutes with an ordinary wooden potato masher, folding the dough over and over. Brush a bowl with melted butter, put in the dough, cover it and stand in a warm place (75° Fahr.) for three or three and a half hours. Form into loaves, put it in square bread pans and when very light bake in a moderately quick oven three-quarters of an hour.

The whey from sour milk makes an exceedingly good bread, and may be used alone, without the addition of water.

If sponged over night, use a third less yeast.

Bread Sticks

Bread sticks are made by rolling ordinary white bread at moulding time into long strips the length and size of a lead pencil. Put them either in a shallow pan or in a bread stick pan, and when very light bake in a quick oven fifteen minutes.

Old Maids

When the bread is ready to mould, break off small bits the size of an English walnut, form them into biscuits, stand them on a cloth and cover with another for about one hour, until they are very light. Bake slowly in muffin rings on a griddle, turning once or twice while baking; or they may be put down into gem pans and when light brushed with sugar and water beaten together. Bake the same as muffins. In some parts of England these are served in place of English muffins. They may be pulled apart and toasted.

Vienna Rolls

Scald one pint of milk, add two level tablespoonfuls of butter and a half teaspoonful of salt, and when lukewarm half a yeast cake, moistened, or onc cupful of home-made yeast. Add sufficient Robin Hood flour to make a soft dough, beating at first, and then kneading; handle it as soft as you can. Put the dough back into a bowl, cover and stand it aside over night. In the morning turn it out carefully on the board, pinch off about a tablespoonful of the dough, make it into a round biscuit, stand on greased baking sheets or in shallow pans, allowing plenty of room for swelling; cover, and when these are very light dip a sharp knife into hot water and cut each biscuit across the top, both ways; brush them with the white of an egg beaten with a tablespoonful of water and bake in a quick oven twenty minutes. If you wish them highly glazed, at the end of twenty minutes draw them from the oven, brush them again quickly with the white of egg and water, and put them back just a moment until brown. These may be made into any of the various shapes for Vienna rolls.

The dough may be rolled out, cut with a good-sized biscuit cutter, one half folded over the other, for pocket book rolls.

English Muffins

Scald one pint of milk, add four level tablespoonfuls of butter or lard; when lukewarm add one yeast cake moistened in a half cupful of water, or a half cupful of yeast, and a half teaspoonful of salt; add one pint of Robin Hood flour, beat thoroughly, then add slowly another half pint of Robin Hood flour, beating all the while; cover and stand aside in a warm place two hours. Heat the griddle slowly, grease the muffin rings and place them over the top, put two tablespoonfuls of the batter in each ring, bake slowly on one side, turn them, rings and all, and bake on the other. As soon as they are sufficiently baked, remove the rings, push them close on the griddle and let them bake slowly for ten minutes. Serve hot, or pull them apart and toast to a rich brown.

Egg Crackers

Sift one quart of Robin Hood flour. Beat the yolks of four eggs and add to them one pint of sweet *cream;* add this to the flour, and beat and knead until smooth. Roll at once into a very thin sheet, cut into round crackers, prick, and bake until a golden brown in a moderately quick oven. Serve warm.

Quick Biscuit

Put one quart of Robin Hood flour into a bowl, add two rounding teaspoonfuls of baking powder, a half teaspoonful of salt, and sift; rub in two level tablespoonfuls of shortening, and add one and a half cupfuls of milk; this quantity is not arbitrary; the dough must be moist, not wet; it may take a little more milk or a little less; add it gradually, wetting always the dry flour. Knead the dough quickly, roll it out, cut it with a small, round cutter, and bake in a quick oven thirty minutes.

Egg Pocket Books

One quart of Robin Hood flour.
One and a half cupfuls of milk.
One egg.
One tablespoonful of butter.
Two teaspoonfuls of baking powder.
Half teaspoonful of salt.

Sift the baking powder and flour, and rub in the butter. Beat the egg, add the milk,

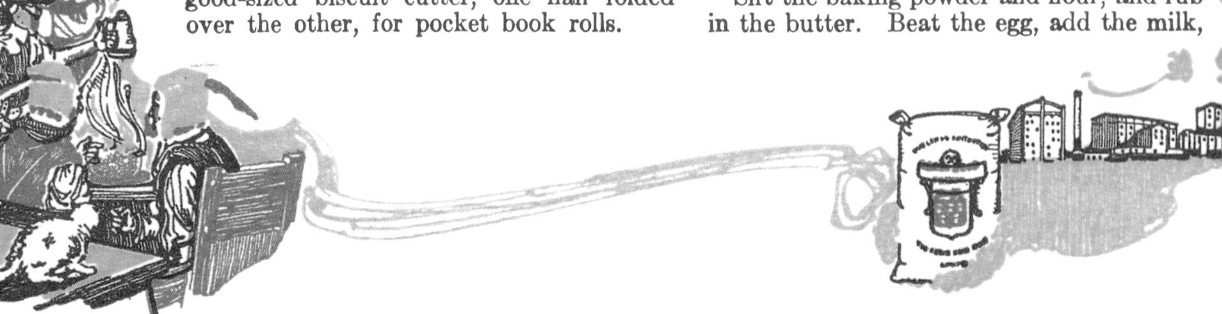

and add this gradually to the flour. The dough must be moist, not wet; roll it out into a sheet a half inch thick, cut with a large, round cutter about four inches in diameter, fold one half of the biscuit over the other, stand in a greased pan, brush the tops of the rolls with milk, and bake in a quick oven a half hour.

These are the nicest of quick hot biscuits.

Oatmeal Brown Bread

One pint of Robin Hood Porridge Oats.
One pint of rolled wheat.
Half pint of granulated yellow cornmeal.
Half pint of Robin Hood flour.
One teaspoonful of baking powder.
Half pint of New Orleans molasses.
One pint of thick, sour milk.
One teaspoonful of salt.

Mix the dry ingredients. Mix the molasses and sour milk; add the soda (dissolved); when this begins to foam stir it in the dry ingredients, mix, turn into a brown bread mould, and boil or steam continuously for four hours; in a fireless cooker, six hours. Lift the lid of the mould and allow the bread to cool in the mould, then turn it out and stand it in a moderately quick oven thirty minutes to dry.

This is quite equal to the best Boston brown bread.

Corn Meal Loaf

Put one pint of milk and a pint of water in a saucepan over the fire; when warm, stir in two-thirds of a cupful of yellow cornmeal, stir until it reaches boiling point, take from the fire and add one pint of milk, a level teaspoonful of salt and a tablespoonful of butter or lard. When the mixture is lukewarm, add one compressed yeast cake, dissolved, or a cupful of home-made yeast; mix thoroughly, and add sufficient Robin Hood flour to make a soft dough; beat thoroughly, cover and stand in a warm place until it doubles its bulk (about two hours and a half). Then, with a limber knife, or spatula, cut in more Robin Hood flour until you have a dough; this dough must be very soft. Do not knead it, but put it at once into square bread pans, cover and stand aside until very light; bake in a moderately quick oven from forty-five minutes to an hour.

Robin Hood Breakfast Wheat Bread

Add one cupful of milk to one cupful of left-over Robin Hood Porridge Wheat; when well mixed, add two eggs (well beaten) and one cupful of Robin Hood flour sifted with two teaspoonfuls of baking powder. Bake in gem pans a half hour.

South Carolina Golden Loaf

Boil three good sized potatoes; when done, drain and press the potatoes through a colander. Scald one pint of milk, add to it two tablespoonfuls of butter, the mashed potatoes, eight tablespoonfuls of sugar, a level teaspoonful of salt, three eggs well beaten, and one compressed yeast cake (moistened) or one cupful of home-made yeast. Stir in sufficient Robin Hood flour to make a batter, beat continuously for five minutes, and continue adding flour, beating and stirring all the while, until you have a soft dough. Knead this on a board until it is light and elastic; it must be soft, but free from stickiness. Put it back in the bowl and stand aside over night. In the morning divide it into loaves, mould each lightly and put them into square bread pans; cover again, and when very light bake in a moderate oven for one hour.

Milk Bread

One pint of milk.
One-half cup of yeast of half a compressed cake.
About two quarts of flour.
One teaspoonful of salt.
One teaspoonful of butter.

Scald the milk and turn it into the bread pan, add the butter and salt. When cool, add the yeast, and sufficient flour to make a thick batter. Beat thoroughly until the batter is full of air-bubbles. Cover, and let it stand in a warm place (72° Fahr.) until morning. Early in the morning add enough flour to make a dough. Take it out on a baking board as soon as it is stiff enough to do so, and knead quickly and gently until the dough is perfectly smooth and elastic, and will not stick to the board or hands. Now put it back in the bread pan, cover, and stand in the same warm place, and let it rise until it doubles its bulk. When light, turn out on the board, divide it into halves, mould lightly into loaves, put them into greased pans, and stand away again until light. Bake in a moderately quick oven (390° Fahr.) for three-quarters of an hour.

Sweet Potato Bread

One quart of Robin Hood flour.
Four roasted sweet potatoes.
One tablespoonful of salt.
One pint of warm water.
One cup of yeast or half a compressed cake.
One tablespoonful of butter.

Put the water into a bread pan or large bowl, add the butter, salt, yeast, and flour; beat well, and stand in a warm place over night. In the morning, bake the potatoes and press them through a sieve into the light sponge, add flour, and finish same as Milk Bread.

Salt-Rising Bread

Add to one pint of scalding water sufficient flour to make a thick batter, add a half teaspoonful of salt, and beat until smooth and full of air bubbles. Cover closely, stand in a pan of warm water and keep in a warm place over night. In the morning, scald one pint of milk, stand aside until lukewarm; add a teaspoonful of salt and enough flour to make a batter that will drop, not pour, from a spoon. Now turn into this the salt rising, which should be very light, and emit a very unpleasant odor; beat thoroughly and continuously for three minutes, then cover with a towel, stand in a pan of warm water, and put where it will keep warm until very light (about two hours); then add sufficient flour to make a dough; knead thoroughly and continuously until smooth and elastic, divide into loaves, mould, place in greased pans, cover with a towel, and, when very light, bake in a moderate oven (300° Fahr.) one hour.

This must be kept very much warmer than a yeast bread, or it will not rise. It is thought by some more digestible than any other kind of bread.

Norwegian Bread

One pint of barley meal.
One-half pint of Graham flour.
One-half pint of Robin Hood wheat flour.
One teaspoonful of salt.
One cup of yeast or half a compressed cake.

Scald the milk and let it stand until lukewarm, then add the salt and yeast, mix, and add all the other ingredients. Beat thoroughly and continuously for ten minutes, then turn into a greased bread pan; cover with paper and stand in a warm place until very light and full of air bubbles, then bake in a moderately quick oven (390° Fahr.) for forty minutes.

Graham Bread

Make a sponge at night as directed in recipe for Milk Bread. In the morning add two large tablespoonfuls of molasses and sufficient Graham flour to make a soft dough. Work well with the hand, mould into loaves, put into well-greased pan, let it rise again, and bake in a moderate oven (300° Fahr.) for one hour.

Graham bread must be watched more carefully than white bread, as it sours quickly.

Boston Brown Bread

Two cups of Yankee rye meal.
One cup of molasses.
One teaspoonful of salt.
Two cups of Indian meal.
One teaspoonful of soda or saleratus.
One and one-half pints of sour milk.

Mix the rye and Indian meal well together. Dissolve the soda or saleratus in two tablespoonfuls of boiling water, then add it to the sour milk; add the molasses, mix, and pour it on the meal, add the salt and mix thoroughly. Pour into a well-greased two-quart brown bread mould, put the lid on, and steam five hours; then remove the lid, put in the oven, and bake thirty minutes.

Southern Rice Bread

Two cups of white Indian meal.
Three eggs.
One and one-quarter pints of milk.
One cup of cold boiled rice.
One ounce of butter, melted.
One teaspoonful of salt.
Two heaping teaspoonfuls baking powder.

Beat the eggs without separating until very light, then add them to the milk; then add the meal, salt, butter, and rice; beat thoroughly, add the baking powder, mix. Grease three round shallow pans, turn in the mixture, put quickly in a hot oven, and bake thirty minutes. Serve hot.

Rye Bread

Make a sponge from wheat flour as directed in recipe for Milk Bread. In the morning add sufficient rye flour to make a soft dough. Knead lightly; then cut the dough in two loaves, mould, place in greased bread pans, cover and stand in a warm place to rise again. When light, bake in a moderate oven (300° Fahr.) for one hour.

Rye bread must not be as stiff as white bread, and does not require so much kneading.

"The Great Flour of Greater Canada"

CEREAL MILL
OATS
ROBIN HOOD FLOUR
ROBIN HOOD MILLS
The

ROBIN HOOD FLOUR
IS DIFFERENT
ROBIN HOOD FLOUR
ROBIN HOOD MILLS

"Home Made Bread from Robin Hood Flour"

"Robin Hood
meeteth a Tanner"

Plain Cakes

Cinnamon Buns

Two ounces of butter.
Three eggs.
Half cupful of good yeast, or
Half a compressed yeast cake.
One pint of milk.
One teaspoonful of salt.
Two tablespoonfuls of sugar.

Scald the milk, and when lukewarm add the salt, sugar, yeast and the butter, melted. Beat the eggs, without separating, add them and sufficient Robin Hood flour to make a thin batter that will drop rather than pour from the spoon. Beat continuously for five minutes, then cover and stand in a warm place over night. In the morning add one cupful of Robin Hood flour, beat thoroughly, and then continue adding flour, stirring and cutting with a limber knife, until you have a soft dough. Cover and stand in a warm place until it has doubled its bulk and is very light, then turn the dough on to a baking board, and without kneading, roll it into a thin sheet; spread lightly with butter, cover thickly with sugar, sprinkle with dried currants, dust with cinnamon and roll in a long roll. Cut this roll into buns of about two inches, place them flat, or cut-side down, closely together, in a round, well-greased pan, cover, stand in a warm place, and when very light bake in a moderately quick oven for three-quarters of an hour.

As sugar burns easily, be careful to protect the bottom of the pan from extreme heat. Turn them from the pan while hot. If properly made, these should be covered with a sort of caramel sauce.

Krapfen

One pint of light bread dough.
Two eggs.
Half cupful of shredded citron or candied orange peel.
One cupful of sugar.
Two ounces, or two tablespoonfuls of butter.
Half grated nutmeg.
Half teaspoonful of cinnamon.

Take the bread dough when it is ready to mould, put it in a large bowl, add the cinnamon, butter, sugar and nutmeg, and break in the eggs. Beat with the hand or a stiff egg-beater until it is free from "strings," then add the fruit, floured, and pour it at once into a greased Turk's-head or round cake pan; cover in a warm place about two hours until very light, and bake three-quarters of an hour in a moderately quick oven.

Bath Buns

One pint of milk.
One cupful of butter.
The yolks of six eggs.
Five cupfuls of sifted Robin Hood flour.
Half cupful of currants.
Half cupful of sugar.
Half cupful of yeast, or
Half a compressed yeast cake.
Half cupful of chopped citron.
One teaspoonful of cinnamon.

Scald the milk, add the butter while hot, and when lukewarm add the yeast, and stir in the flour, beating all the while; cover and stand in a warm place (about 70° Fahr.) until morning. Then add the sugar and the yolks of the eggs beaten together, and the currants and citron, floured; work carefully with the hand, adding sufficient flour to make a soft dough; when smooth, roll out and cut with a round cutter. Stand the buns in greased pans, cover, set away in a warm place until they are very light, then bake in a quick oven thirty-five minutes. When the buns are done, brush the tops with the white of an egg, a tablespoonful of milk and a tablespoonful of sugar beaten together; run them back in the oven until they are glossy brown.

Spanish Bun

Quarter pound of butter.
Half pound of sugar.
Half pound of currants.
Three eggs.
Half pint of milk.
One cupful of yeast, or
One compressed yeast cake.
One teaspoonful of cinnamon.
One nutmeg, grated.
Quarter teaspoonful of mace.
One pound of Robin Hood flour.
Half teaspoonful of salt.

Scald the milk, take it from the fire and add the butter, cut into dice. Beat the eggs, without separating, until they are very light, add the sugar, beat again, add them to the milk; when lukewarm, add the yeast and spices, and stir in the Robin Hood flour; beat and work very carefully. This dough must be very soft, almost a pouring batter. Stir in the currants, well floured, pour into a square baking pan, cover, and stand in a warm place four or five hours until very light, then bake in a moderately quick oven one hour. When done, turn the bun from the pan, dust it thickly with powdered sugar and serve while fresh, not hot.

At low altitude more butter can be used in all these cakes.

Moravian Sugar Cake

Half pound of brown sugar.
One pint of milk.
Two eggs.
Half cup of yeast or half of a compressed cake.
Six ounces of butter.
Three pints of Robin Hood flour.
Two tablespoonfuls of powdered cinnamon.
One teaspoonful of salt.

Cut four ounces of the butter into small pieces, add it to the milk, turn into a farina boiler, and stir over the fire until the milk is scalding hot and the butter melted. Sift the flour into a large bowl. When the milk is lukewarm, add the yeast and salt. Make a well in the centre of the flour, pour into it the milk, and stir in sufficient flour to make a thin batter; cover, and set in a warm place until very light (this will take about two hours and a half). When light, add the eggs well beaten, half the cinnamon, and half the sugar; then stir in the remainder of the flour. Beat it very hard, pour into a greased, shallow, baking pan and set it again to rise. Mix the remaining sugar and cinnamon until smooth and light. When the cake is light, make deep holes at equal distances all over it, filling each hole as soon as it is made with a teaspoonful of the paste. Dust the cake heavily with powdered sugar, and bake in a moderately quick oven one hour.

Bread Cake

One pint of bread dough.
One cup of sugar.
Two eggs.
Two ounces of butter.
One teaspoonful of vanilla.

Take the dough at the second kneading, put it into a large bowl, and add all the other ingredients. Beat with the hand until smooth and free from strings, then turn into a greased pan, cover, and stand in a warm place (72° Fahr.) until light (this will take about two hours). Bake in a moderately quick oven about three-quarters of an hour.

Spanish Bun

Half pound of butter.
Half pound of sugar.
Half pound of currants.
Three eggs.
Half pint of cream.
One gill of yeast.
One teaspoonful of cinnamon.
One nutmeg, grated.
Quarter teaspoonful of mace.
One pound of Robin Hood flour.

Warm the cream gently, take it from the fire, add the butter cut into dice. Beat the eggs until very light, stir them into the cream; then add the sugar, slowly, stirring all the time; then add the flour, spices, and yeast; give a thorough beating, and add the currants well floured. Pour into a square baking pan, well greased (the batter should be about one inch thick), cover, and stand in a warm place to rise for four or five hours. When it has doubled its bulk, place in a moderately quick oven, and bake one hour. When done, turn from the pan, dust with powdered sugar, and use while fresh.

FANCY CAKES

In cake making success follows those who are attentive to detail. These recipes are written for high altitude; at sea level the quantity of butter may be doubled and a third more sugar used. Layer cakes are best for altitude as richness can be given in the filling.

Measure everything carefully before beginning.

Fine granulated sugar makes the best cake.

Measure the flour after sifting.

Round the teaspoonfuls of baking powder against the side of the can as you draw it out. A teaspoonful to a cupful of flour is the usual proportion. If you use cream of tartar and soda, one teaspoonful of cream of tartar to each half teaspoonful of soda.

Lard, oil or suet is best to grease cake pans. Butter usually sticks and burns easily.

Have the oven ready the moment the cake is mixed.

If your cake browns as soon as you put it in the oven, the oven is too hot; cool it quickly by lifting the lid of the stove; if you use gas, turn out one row of burners.

Do not move the cake in the oven until the centre is thoroughly "set," or it will fall.

When you look at the cake while baking, do it as quickly as possible, and shut the door carefully.

In the following recipes the time required for baking is given as nearly as possible, but never take a cake out unless you are sure it is done. If you have doubts, put it to your ear; if it ticks, put it back. Or try it in the centre with a broom splint; if no dough adheres, the cake is done.

For measuring, use cups of uniform size. It is better to use the ordinary kitchen measuring cup, which holds a half pint.

Never melt the butter for cakes; warm it slightly and beat it to a cream.

Chocolate Cake

Two ounces or two squares of chocolate.
Four eggs.
Half cupful of milk.
Quarter cupful or two tablespoonfuls of butter.
One cupful of sugar.
Two cupfuls of Robin Hood flour.
One teaspoonful of vanilla.
Two rounding teaspoonfuls of baking powder.

Dissolve the chocolate in five tablespoonfuls of boiling water. Beat the butter to a cream, add gradually the sugar, add the yolks, and when light add the melted chocolate, milk and the flour and baking powder sifted together; give the whole a vigorous beating, and then stir in carefully the well-beaten whites of the eggs, and the vanilla. Turn into three shallow layer cake pans and bake in a moderately quick oven about thirty-five minutes. Put together with nut filling.

Devil's Food

One egg.
One cupful of sugar.
Two ounces of chocolate.
Two-thirds of a cupful of milk.
Quarter cupful of butter.
One and a half cupfuls of Robin Hood flour.
Two rounding teaspoonfuls of baking powder.
One teaspoonful of vanilla.

Grate the chocolate into the milk, and stir it over the fire until it is thoroughly melted. Beat the butter to a cream, add the egg, beaten without separating, and the sugar; when light, add the chocolate mixture, and then stir in the flour and baking powder, sifted. Bake in two layers and put together with caramel filling.

Grafton Cake

Four level tablespoonfuls of butter.
One cupful of sugar.
Two eggs.
One cupful of water.
Two and a half cupfuls of Robin Hood flour.
Two rounding teaspoonfuls of baking powder.
Quarter of a grated nutmeg.

Beat the yolks, sugar and butter together until light. Sift the baking powder and flour. Measure the water. Add the water and flour alternately, beat thoroughly, add the nutmeg and stir in the beaten whites of the eggs. In a loaf cake bake three-quarters of an hour; in three layers, a half hour. Put together with an ordinary cream filling, or melted marshmallows.

Fancy Cakes
Continued

Hazelnut Cake

One cupful of sugar.
Four eggs.
One cupful of Robin Hood flour.
One rounding teaspoonful of baking powder.
One teaspoonful of ground cinnamon.
Half teaspoonful of ground allspice.

Separate the eggs, beat the yolks and sugar, add the well-beaten white, the spices, and the flour and baking powder (sifted). Bake in two layers. While this is baking, make a

Hazelnut Filling

One cupful of milk.
One level tablespoonful of cornstarch.
Two eggs.
Half cupful of sugar.
Half cupful of hazelnuts, chopped fine.
One teaspoonful of vanilla.

Heat the milk, add the cornstarch, moistened, and when thick add the eggs and sugar beaten together. Take from the fire, and when cool add the vanilla and nuts. This should be sufficiently thick to hold its shape. When the cake and mixture are cold, put all the filling between the layers, dust the top thickly with powdered sugar, and serve.

Molasses Cake

One cupful of New Orleans molasses.
One tablespoonful of butter.
One cupful of boiling water.
One teaspoonful of baking soda.
Two and a half cupfuls of Robin Hood flour.
One tablespoonful of ginger.

Dissolve the soda in a tablespoonful of warm water, add it to the molasses, add the butter, boiling water, ginger, and then stir in the flour; bake in a shallow baking pan in a moderate oven forty-five minutes.

Spice Cake

One cupful of brown sugar.
Half cupful of molasses.
One teaspoonful of baking soda.
One tablespoonful of cinnamon.
One cupful of sour cream.
One tablespoonful of allspice.
One pound of raisins.
Three cupfuls of Robin Hood flour.

Chop the raisins. Dissolve the soda in a tablespoonful of warm water, add it to the molasses, add the cream, sugar and flour, beat thoroughly, and add the spices and the raisins. Bake in a square bread pan in a moderate oven one hour.

This is my every-day cake. If I am without thick, sour cream, I use one cupful of sour milk with a tablespoonful of olive oil. If properly made, it passes very well for ordinary fruit cake.

English Walnut Cake

Quarter cupful of butter.
Two cupfuls of Robin Hood flour.
The whites of four eggs.
One cupful of sugar.
Half cupful of water.
One cupful of English walnut or hickory-nut kernels.
Two rounding teaspoonfuls of baking powder.

Beat the butter and sugar to a cream, add the water, and the flour sifted with the baking powder, alternately. Add half the well-beaten whites, then the nuts, chopped, then the remainder of the whites. Pour into a square, flat pan lined with buttered paper, and bake in a moderate oven three-quarters of an hour. Ice and garnish with nuts.

Angel's Food

The whites of seven eggs.
One cupful of fine granulated sugar.
Two-thirds of a cupful of Robin Hood flour.
One teaspoonful of flavoring
One teaspoonful of cream of tartar.

Sift the flour five times. Sift the sugar. Beat the whites of the eggs to a very stiff froth, add the cream of tartar, beat again, add the sugar, sift in carefully the flour, and at last add the flavoring. Turn quickly into an ungreased pan and bake in a moderate oven forty-five to fifty minutes. When the cake is done, turn the pan upside down and allow the cake to cool; when cool, loosen around the edges with a knife and it will fall out.

Sunshine Cake

For this, follow the recipe for Angel's Food. Add the yolks of four eggs to the whites after you have added the cream of tartar and beaten them very stiff.

Fancy Cakes
Continued

Sponge Cake

Six eggs.
The weight of the eggs in sugar.
Half the weight of the eggs in Robin Hood flour.
The juice and grated rind of one lemon.

Put the eggs, instead of weights, on your weighing machine, and balance them with sugar; then balance half with flour. Separate the eggs, beat the yolks and sugar for fifteen minutes until very light, then add the lemon rind and juice; fold in carefully the well-beaten whites and sift in lightly the flour. Pour into a greased sponge cake pan and bake forty-five minutes.

Fruit Cake

Ten eggs.
One pound of sugar.
Half pound of butter.
One and a half pounds of currants.
One and a half pounds of raisins.
Three-quarters of a pound of citron.
One pound of Robin Hood flour.
One teaspoonful of allspice.
Half teaspoonful of cloves.
One teaspoonful of cinnamon.
One nutmeg, grated.
The grated rind of one orange and one lemon.
If you use it, a half cupful of brandy.

Beat the eggs, without separating, until light. Beat the butter and sugar together, add the eggs, then the spices and the flour, when light add all the fruit, mixed and floured; add the rind of the lemon and orange, and the brandy; if you do not use brandy, use orange or grape juice. Line two round fruit-cake pans with greased paper, pour in the mixture and bake in a moderate oven four hours. This will make one eight-pound cake or two four-pound cakes.

You will find the cakes will keep longer and be more moist if they are steamed two hours and baked two hours.

Never-Fail Cake

Quarter cupful of butter.
One and a half cupfuls of sugar.
One cupful of milk.
The whites of five eggs.
Two and a half cupfuls of Robin Hood flour.
Two rounding teaspoonfuls of baking powder.

Cream the butter and sugar. Sift the baking powder and flour, add them alternately with the milk to the sugar, beat thoroughly, fold in the well-beaten whites and bake in three layers, or one loaf cake.

Mocha Cake

Four eggs.
One cupful of powdered sugar.
One cupful of Robin Hood flour.

Separate the eggs, beat the yolks and sugar fifteen minutes; add a tablespoonful of lemon juice and half the grated rind of a lemon. Sift the flour before you measure it, then sift it with a level teaspoonful of baking powder. Beat the whites of the eggs to a stiff froth; add them alternately with the flour. Bake in two layers, and when cold put together with caramel filling.

Hermits

Half cupful of butter.
One cupful of sugar.
Two eggs.
A saltspoonful of baking soda.
One teaspoonful of cinnamon.
One saltspoonful of cloves.
Quarter of a nutmeg, grated.
One cupful of seeded raisins.
Sufficient Robin Hood flour to make a batter.

Cream the butter, add the sugar and the eggs, beaten without separating. Dissolve the soda in a tablespoonful of water and add it to the mixture; add all the spices and the raisins, then stir in the flour. The batter must be sufficiently thick to drop from a spoon. Drop in a shallow greased pan and bake in a moderate oven fifteen or twenty minutes.

Cookies

Three cupfuls of brown sugar.
Quarter cupful of butter and lard.
One cupful of cold water.
Two rounding teaspoonfuls of baking powder.
Half a grated nutmeg.

Beat the butter and lard and the sugar, and add the water. Sift the baking powder with two cupfuls of Robin Hood flour, add the nutmeg, mix until sufficiently stiff to roll; add more flour if necessary. Sprinkle the board with granulated sugar, roll out the dough, cut, and bake in a moderately quick oven until a golden brown.

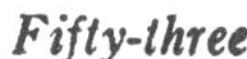

Fancy Cakes
Continued

Maple Cake

Make a Grafton cake and bake it in three layers; when the cake is done and cool, put it together with the following filling:

Boil two cupfuls of maple sugar, a half cupful of cream and a tablespoonful of butter together until it is the consistency to spread; stir carefully to prevent burning. Take from the fire, flavor with vanilla, and cool.

Jackson Snaps

Half cupful of butter.
One cupful of sugar.
One egg.
One cupful of water.
About three cupfuls of Robin Hood flour.
Juice and grated rind of one lemon.

Cream the butter, add the sugar, then the egg, well beaten, and water; stir in carefully the flour. When the dough is sufficiently stiff to roll out, roll it in a thin sheet, cut with a small round cutter and bake in a moderately quick oven until a light brown.

Ginger or cinnamon may be added if desired.

Cream Puffs

Half pint of water.
One ounce of butter.
One cupful of Robin Hood flour (four ounces).
Four eggs.

Put the water and butter over the fire in a saucepan; when it boils throw in hastily the flour, stir quickly until you have a smooth, thick dough, and stand aside until cool. Then break in one egg, beat until well mixed; then add another egg, beat again, and so on until you have all the eggs added; at last beat for five minutes, cover and stand the dough in a warm place for an hour. Drop by tablespoonfuls on lightly-greased tins, leaving a space of two inches between each puff; bake in a very quick oven. In a half hour pick them up; if they are light and perfectly hollow, they are done; if heavy, bake longer. When cold make a slit in the side of each and fill with a thick, rich, soft custard, or whipped cream.

Chocolate éclairs are made from cream puff batter, pressed through a plain pastry tube into the desired shape. They are filled with custard and iced with chocolate icing.

Oatmeal Wafers

Quarter cupful of butter.
One cupful of sugar.
One egg.
A level teaspoonful of baking soda.
Two tablespoonfuls of milk.
Robin Hood Porridge Oats.

Beat the butter to a cream, add the egg, well beaten, and gradually work in the sugar. Dissolve the soda in a tablespoonful of water, add it to the sugar and milk, and work in sufficient dry oatmeal to make a very stiff dough; this will take two or two and a half cupfuls. Knead until the mixture will hold together, roll into a very thin sheet, cut into squares like Graham crackers, and bake in a shallow pan, in a moderate oven until a light brown, dry and crisp; this should take ten or twelve minutes.

If well made, these are equal to, if not better than, Graham crackers.

Cake Without Eggs

One and a half cups of sugar.
Two cups of Robin Hood flour.
One teaspoonful of baking powder.
One cup of milk.
Two tablespoonfuls (or two ounces) of butter.
One teaspoonful of flavoring.

Beat the butter and sugar to a cream, add the milk and flour, and beat vigorously; add the salt, flavoring and baking powder; mix well, and bake in a moderate oven about thirty minutes.

Buttermilk Cake

One cup of butter.
Three cups of sugar.
Five cups of Robin Hood flour.
Two cups of buttermilk.
Half teaspoonful of soda or saleratus.
Four eggs.

Beat the butter to a cream, then add the sugar and the yolks of the eggs; beat again until very light. Mash the soda or saleratus, add it to the buttermilk, stir until dissolved, then add to the other mixture. Add the flour, beat until smooth, then stir in quickly the well-beaten whites. Bake in a moderate oven about three-quarters of an hour.

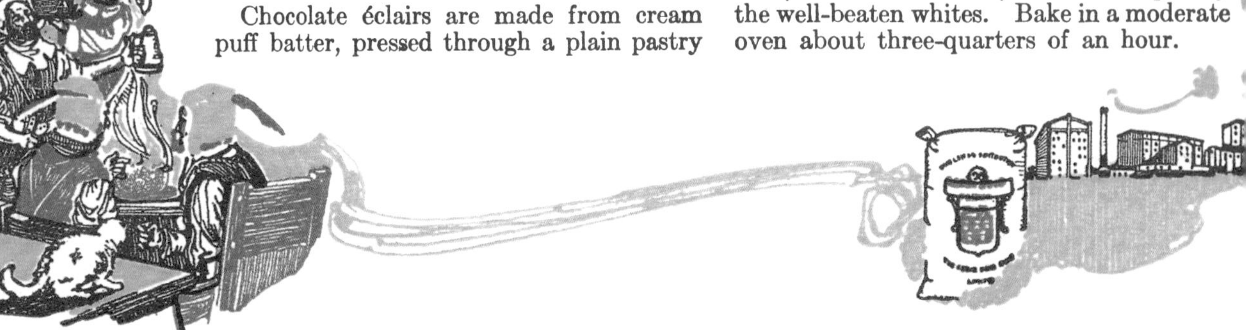

Indian Loaf Cake

One pound of Indian meal.
Quarter pound of raisins.
Half pound of sugar.
Quarter pound of butter.
Quarter pound of currants.
Two eggs.

Cut the butter into the meal, and pour over it sufficient boiling milk to make a stiff batter. Beat the eggs all together until very light. When the batter is cool, add the eggs and sugar. Seed the raisins; wash, pick and dry the currants; mix the fruit and flour them well, stir them into the batter, and bake in a very slow oven two hours.

Dried Fruit Cake

Three cups of dried apples or any other dried fruit.
Three-quarters cup of butter.
One cup of sugar.
One teaspoonful of cinnamon.
Two cups of molasses.
Two eggs.
One cup of milk.
One teaspoonful of soda.
Half teaspoonful of cloves.
Half nutmeg, grated.

Soak the fruit over night in cold water. Then chop it slightly, and simmer in the molasses for two hours. Beat the eggs and sugar together until light, then add the butter; beat again, add the fruit, milk, spices, soda dissolved in a tablespoonful of boiling water, sufficient flour to make a stiff batter that will drop from the spoon. Bake in a very moderate oven for two hours.

Sponge Cake

Six eggs.
Weight of the eggs in sugar.
Half the weight of the eggs in Robin Hood flour.
Juice and rind of one lemon.

After weighing the sugar and flour, separate the eggs. Beat the yolks and sugar together until very light. Now add the juice and rind of the lemon and half the flour. Beat the whites to a very stiff froth, add half of them to the cake, then the remaining half of the flour, and then the remaining half of the whites; stir lightly, and pour into a greased cake pan. Bake in a quick oven forty-five minutes.

Soft Gingerbread

Three cups of Robin Hood flour.
Half cup of milk.
Half cup of lard.
One and one-half cups of molasses.
One teaspoonful of soda.
Two eggs.
One tablespoonful of ginger.

Beat the yolks of the eggs and the lard together; then add the milk, soda and molasses; add the ginger and flour. Beat the whites to a stiff froth, add them carefully. Bake in a moderate oven for three-quarters of an hour.

Plain Cup Cake

Half cup of butter.
One and one-half cups of sugar.
One cup of milk or water.
Three cups of Robin Hood flour.
Juice and rind of a lemon.
Four eggs.
Two teaspoonfuls of baking powder.

Beat the butter, sugar and yolks of the eggs together until light; then add the water or milk, and half the flour, and beat until smooth; then add the well-beaten whites, then the remainder of the flour, then the juice and rind of the lemon and the baking powder. Mix thoroughly and bake in a greased Turk's-head, in a moderate oven, about three-quarters of an hour.

Layer Cake

Half pound of butter.
Five eggs.
Six ounces of Robin Hood flour.
Quarter teaspoonful of mace.
Half pound of sugar.
Two ounces of cornstarch.
One teaspoonful of vanilla.
Two tablespoonfuls of sherry.
One teaspoonful of baking powder.

Beat the butter to a cream; add the sugar gradually, beating all the while, then add the yolks of the eggs, then the well-beaten whites, then the flour, cornstarch and baking powder; beat well; add the flavorings, mix well. Grease three deep jelly tins, pour in the cake, and bake in a moderately quick oven fifteen minutes. When done remove, carefully from the pans, and stand them on a towel for a few minutes to cool.

ICINGS AND FILLINGS

Icings and Fillings

Boiled Icing

Boil one cupful of granulated sugar, a saltspoonful of cream of tartar and a half cupful of water together until they spin a thread, pour while hot into the well-beaten whites of two eggs, beat until it is thick enough to spread without running; flavor with vanilla, orange, lemon or maple flavoring.

If it remains thin, you have not boiled the sugar and water sufficiently long. If it is too stiff, you have boiled it a little too much. After a single trial you can gauge this exactly.

For Nut Filling, add chopped nuts.

For Fruit Filling, add chopped candied fruit.

Chocolate Icing

Beat the whites of two eggs, adding gradually ten ounces of sifted icing sugar, beat until stiff enough to form a pyramid, add two ounces of melted Baker's chocolate and use.

Chocolate Icing Number Two

Quarter pound of grated chocolate.
Quarter pound of powdered sugar.
One tablespoonful of water.
One teaspoonful of vanilla.

Put the chocolate in a saucepan, stand it in another of boiling water, add the sugar and water and stir until smooth; take from the fire, add the vanilla and it is ready for use.

Orange Icing

Half pound of powdered sugar.
One tablespoonful of boiling water.
The grated rind of one orange.
Sufficient orange juice to moisten.

Put the sugar in a bowl, add the rind, mix thoroughly and add the water; stir, and if this is too thick to spread, add a little orange juice. This will harden at once, and is exceedingly nice for small cakes.

Boiled Chocolate Filling

One and a half cupfuls of sugar.
Half a cupful of milk.
One teaspoonful of butter.
One teaspoonful of vanilla.
Two squares of Baker's chocolate.

Put all the ingredients, except the vanilla, into a saucepan; boil, stirring all the time, ten minutes. Take from the fire, add the vanilla and beat until a consistency to spread.

Caramel Filling

One and a half cupfuls of brown sugar.
Half a cupful of cream.
Two tablespoonfuls of milk.
One tablespoonful of caramel.

Put all the ingredients in a saucepan and boil until a soft ball can be formed, when a little of the mixture is dropped in cold water; this will take one-half hour or a little more. Stand the saucepan in a pan of cold water and beat until the right consistency to spread.

All these icings will answer for frostings of fillings.

Plain Icing

Whites of two eggs.
One teaspoonful of lemon juice.
Half pound of powdered sugar.

Place the eggs in a refrigerator or some very cold place one hour before using. Break them carefully and beat the whites until frothy, then sift the sugar in gradually, beating all the while; add the lemon juice, and continue the beating until the icing is fine and white, and stiff enough to stand alone. Keep in a cool place until wanted. Spread with a knife dipped in ice-water. If ornaments are used, they must be placed on the cake while the ice is still moist. This may be varied by adding different flavorings, such as strawberry, pineapple, rose, vanilla, etc.

Strawberry icing should always be colored with a few drops of cochineal.

Gelatin Icing

Put one even tablespoonful of gelatin into a bowl, cover it with one tablespoonful of cold water, let it soak half an hour; then add two tablespoonfuls of boiling water, stir until dissolved, then add pulverized sugar to make the mixture a proper consistency to spread. Flavor to taste. Let the cake cool, spread the icing quickly over it, and stand in a cool place to dry.

"Robin Hood dineth & the Bishop"

Pastry & Pies

PASTRY AND PIES

Good pastry requires good flour and good shortening. For French paste use only butter. For plain paste use half butter and half lard, or all lard. *All* paste must be quickly made in a cold place.

French Puff Paste

One pound of sifted Robin Hood flour.
One pound of good butter.
One teaspoonful of salt.
One teaspoonful of sugar.
The white of one egg.
One cupful of ice water.

Scald a bowl, and cool with cold water. Wash your hands in soap suds, rinse them in cold water but do not dry them; this is done to prevent the butter from sticking. Fill the bowl partly full of cold water, put in the butter, break it apart and work it with the hands under the water until it becomes soft and elastic. The water must be very cold. If your hands get too cold, dip them in hot water for a moment and go on washing the butter. The butter must not become too soft, nor must it stick to the hands. Put the flour on a marble slab or in the centre of a large meat platter, make a well in the centre and put in a lump of the washed butter the size of an egg. Put in the white of the egg, sugar and salt. Work this with the thumb and two fingers to a paste, adding gradually the ice water, and gradually work in all the flour. When the flour is worked in and you have a good stiff dough, knead it as you would bread for five minutes, then cut it into halves and roll each half into a sheet. Roll or pat the butter into a thin sheet, break it off in bits and lay it over one sheet of dough, dust this thickly with flour, cover it with the other sheet, pound lightly with a rolling pin and roll from you into a long thin sheet; fold in the sides, then the ends, then turn it around so that the fold will run to and from you; roll from you again, fold as before, place it on a pie dish and stand it in a cold place, or on the ice, for fifteen minutes. Then dust the board with flour, and roll and fold it in the same manner twice more, and stand it on the ice for fifteen minutes. Do this until you have rolled it from six to eight times. Then dust a napkin with flour, put in the paste, fold over the napkin, put it in a pie dish and stand it in a cold place, or on the ice, over night, and it is ready for use.

A novice will make better paste by rolling it six rather than eight times.

To Bake a Puff Paste

Perhaps the most important part of good puff paste is the baking. If you roll it too much, so that it becomes soft, it is bound to toughen and harden in the baking. The paste must be icy cold when it is put in the hot oven. Roll and cut the patties, put them on a baking sheet or pan and stand away on the ice; when the oven is hot (about 450° to 460° Fahr.) put in the paste. It is difficult to bake puff paste in high altitudes; it is apt to melt and run out of shape. To insure success, use a chemical thermometer and let it register at least 460°; at sea level, 400° Fahr. will be better. Have a strong under-heat, so that the patties will rise their full height before browning.

To Make Patties

Roll puff paste into a sheet a quarter of an inch thick, and cut it into rounds with a large round cutter. With a smaller cutter, take the centres from two-thirds of the rounds. Brush the solid round with beaten egg, put on top one round, put on one of the cut rounds, brush with white of egg, and put on another circle. This makes one solid round with two circles on top. Lift this carefully to your baking pan, and so continue until all the patties are made. Stand aside for at least one hour, until very cold.

Plain Paste with Butter

Have everything as cold as possible. In warm weather stand the butter and flour in the refrigerator for several hours before using them. Sift Robin Hood flour and measure carefully three cupfuls; put it in a large mixing bowl, add a teaspoonful of salt, a teaspoonful of sugar and a half pound of butter. With a sharp knife cut the butter into small pieces in the flour, add one cupful of ice water, gradually lifting with a knife the portion which you have moistened first, and push it to one side; then wet another portion, and so continue until the paste is moist, not wet. Then cut it together until you can lift it from the bowl with a knife. Dredge the baking board with flour, turn out the paste and roll it lightly and quickly from you into a long, thin sheet. Fold in the sides, then the ends, turn the paste around and roll it quickly from you again, fold and roll again, fold it, put it in a napkin, put it on a pan, and stand it on the ice or in a cold place.

A Word of Caution: Add the water very carefully, mixing the paste with a knife. Do not pour the water twice in the same place, but be particular to always wet the dry flour. This is ready to use as soon as cold, and if well made is almost as light as puff paste, and like puff paste, must be baked at high altitude in a very hot oven.

Every-day Paste

Sift one quart of Robin Hood flour, add a half cupful of lard, a teaspoonful of salt and a cupful of ice water; mix the salt and flour, put in the lard, and with the tips of the fingers rub it quickly into the flour. Add a little water at a time until the paste is moist; it should take nearly a cupful. Knead quickly into a loaf, roll it out in a sheet and roll it up; stand aside until quite cold and it is ready for use.

Apple Tart

Pare, quarter and core six tart apples; cut each quarter into halves, put them in a deep baking dish and put over a half cupful of sugar, the juice of half a lemon if you have it, and a half cupful of water. Cut a tablespoonful of butter into bits and place them over the top. Roll plain paste in a thin sheet, put it over the top, make a hole in the centre, brush the paste with a little milk or beaten egg, and bake in a quick oven until the apples are tender (about three-quarters of an hour). Apple sauce may be used in the place of raw apples.

Peaches may be substituted for apples and used in the same way.

Cherry Pie

Line a pie dish with good plain paste, fill it with stoned cherries, sprinkle over six tablespoonfuls of sugar, dredge lightly with flour, cover with the upper crust rolled as thin as possible, trim the edges neatly with a knife, make a small vent in the centre, press the edges tightly together so that the juice of the fruit will not run out while baking, and bake in a quick oven a half hour.

Cocoanut Custard

Beat two eggs with a half cupful of sugar until very light, then add one pint of milk, half a nutmeg, grated, and two cupfuls of grated cocoanut. Line two pie dishes with paste, fill with the cocoanut mixture and bake in a quick oven thirty to forty minutes. The custard must be "set" in the centre. It takes longer in high altitude than at sea level.

Lemon Meringue

Beat the yolks of three eggs and one cupful of sugar together until light, add the grated yellow rind and juice of one lemon. Put two level tablespoonfuls of Robin Hood flour into a cup, add a little milk, mix until smooth, then fill the cup with milk, strain this through a sieve into the eggs and sugar and mix thoroughly. Line a deep pie plate with good paste, putting an extra rim of two layers of paste around the edge, pour in the mixture and bake in a hot oven until the custard is "set" (forty-five minutes at high altitude, thirty minutes at sea level). Beat the whites of the eggs until stiff, add one tablespoonful of powdered sugar at high altitude, three tablespoonfuls at sea level, and beat until stiff and glossy. When the pies are done, take them from the oven, put the meringue, by spoonfuls, over the top, dust thickly with powdered sugar and brown lightly in the oven. Serve cold the same day on which they are baked.

Cranberry Tart

Line a pie dish with plain paste, put an extra rim around the edge, fill the dish with mashed cranberries, cover over half as much sugar as you have cranberries, and bake in a quick oven until the cranberries are clear and transparent, about a half hour.

Pumpkin Pie

Pare and cut the pumpkin in pieces about one inch square; put them into a stewing pan with just enough water to keep them from burning; stew slowly until tender (about half an hour), then press through a colander. To every half pint of pumpkin, add a piece of butter the size of a walnut, and a quarter-teaspoonful of salt; mix, and let stand until cold. When cold, put one pint of this pumpkin into a large bowl, add to it one pint of milk, a half-teaspoonful of ground mace, the same of ground cinnamon, and one teaspoonful of ground ginger; mix all well together and sweeten to taste. Beat four eggs until light, then add them to the mixture. Line four deep pie plates with good plain paste, fill with this mixture, and bake in a quick oven (400° Fahr.) for about thirty minutes.

The Kershaw pumpkin is best for pies.

If you use liquor, a gill of brandy may be added to the recipe given.

Mince Meat

Cover two pounds of lean beef with boiling water, boil rapidly five minutes, put it in a fireless cooker if you have one, and stand it aside over night; without a fireless cooker, cook slowly two and a half to three hours, until tender, and stand aside to cool. Shred and chop fine two pounds of beef suet. Pare, core and chop four pounds of apples. Shred one pound of citron. Stone two pounds of layer raisins, or use the ordinary seedless raisins. Chop the meat, put it in a large pan, add the suet, apples, raisins, two pounds of currants; add the citron, two pounds of sugar, two pounds of sultanas, a half pound of candied lemon peel, shredded, a quarter of an ounce of ground cloves, two nutmegs, grated, a half ounce of ground cinnamon, a tablespoonful of salt, and the juice and grated rind of two oranges and two lemons. Mix thoroughly and pack into a good sized stone jar; pour over one quart of good brandy and one quart of sherry; cover closely and stand aside in a cold place to keep all winter. When needed for use, dip out the desired quantity and thin it with cider.

Fresh beef's tongue, or the heart, or the round of beef, or the sticking piece may be used.

Farina Flourindine

Put one pint of milk in a double boiler, when hot stir in four level tablespoonfuls of Robin Hood Farina, stir until the milk thickens; take from the fire, add the yolks of three eggs beaten with a half cupful of sugar; add a teaspoonful of vanilla and stand aside to cool. Line two good sized pie dishes with plain paste, cover the bottoms thickly with seeded raisins, pour over the farina mixture and bake in a hot oven until the custard is "set" (about forty-five minutes). While these are baking, make a meringue by beating the whites of the eggs to a stiff froth, add a tablespoonful of powdered sugar, beat until fine and dry, take the pies from the oven, spread the meringue over, making it smooth, dust with powdered sugar and brown quickly in the oven.

Italian Pie

Beat three eggs, without separating, for fifteen minutes; add five tablespoonfuls of powdered sugar, beat five minutes, add a half cupful of finely chopped almonds, two tablespoonfuls of cocoa or grated chocolate, and sprinkle in slowly two-thirds of a cupful of dry, sifted bread crumbs. Line a square pan, putting a rim of extra paste around the edge, pour in the mixture and bake in a moderately quick oven, about 360°, for a half hour. At sea level watch this carefully to prevent scorching. It must be "set" in the centre. Serve cold. Cut into strips one inch wide, the width of the pan.

Italian Meringue

Roll good plain or puff paste into a thin sheet, cut with a sharp knife or pastry jagger into pieces four inches long and two inches wide; put these in a baking pan or sheet, pick lightly with a steel fork and bake in a quick oven until they are thoroughly done; at high altitude this takes three-quarters of an hour. When cool spread lightly with raspberry or gooseberry jam, cover with a meringue made from the whites of three eggs, dust the meringue thickly with chopped nuts and put in the oven a moment to brown.

Banbury Tarts

Chop a half pound of seeded raisins, add a half cupful of sugar, one egg slightly beaten, a half cupful of bread or cracker crumbs, and the juice and grated rind of a lemon. Roll plain paste into a thin sheet, cut quickly, either with a sharp knife or a pastry jagger, into pieces about four inches long and three inches wide. Put a tablespoonful of the mixture on each piece, brush the edges quickly with water, fold one half over the other, press the edges together, pick the top with a steel fork, stand them at once in a baking pan, and when very cold bake in a quick oven thirty minutes; at sea level have the oven moderately hot and bake the same length of time.

Napoleons

I never have tried to make Napoleons at high altitude, but I fancy they could be quite easily done. Roll puff paste into a very thin sheet, cut the sheet into three squares, making them as large as you can; pick the sheets and put them into baking pans in a quick oven to bake. When done, take them from the oven and put them aside to cool. While they are baking and cooling put a cupful of milk into a double boiler, add a tablespoonful of cornstarch (moistened); when this is smooth and thick add the yolks of two eggs beaten with two tablespoonfuls of sugar, cook a minute, take from the fire, add a teaspoonful of vanilla and stand this aside to cool. At serving time put down one sheet of the baked paste, cover with a layer of the raspberry jam, spread another sheet with the cream filling, put it on top of the one with the raspberry jam, put on the remaining sheet and cover with ordinary icing. Use while fresh.

Oyster Patties

One batch of puff paste.
One pint of milk or cream.
One tablespoonful of cornstarch.
Twenty-five nice fat oysters.
One tablespoonful of butter.
Salt and pepper to taste.

Roll out the puff paste about one inch thick. Then, with a round tin cutter, cut out a patty and lay it on a greased tin sheet. Brush it lightly over the top with the beaten yolk of an egg, being careful not to allow any of the yolk to run down the sides, as it cements the edges together and prevents it from being light; then take a cutter, two sizes smaller, and press it in the centre and nearly through the patty, and so on until you have the whole cut. Now put them on the ice for a half-hour, or until the oven is very hot (400° Fahr.). Then bake about twenty minutes, or until a nice brown. The inside cut acts as a non-conductor, and prevents the heat from reaching the centre, consequently all the paste inside this ring should be unbaked. Now remove the lid crust carefully, and save it for the lid of the patty. Take out this unbaked portion with a spoon. Put the patties back in the oven for ten minutes; leave the door open, as they only want a little drying. Now put the oysters on to boil, in their own liquor; as soon as they boil, drain them. Put the milk or cream on to boil in a farina boiler. Rub the butter and cornstarch together until smooth, and add to the boiling milk or cream; stir until it boils, add salt and pepper, and last, the oysters; let boil up again and take from the fire.

TO FILL THE PATTIES

Put two oysters and a little sauce in each one, put on the lid, and serve.

Cranberry Pie

Line a pie dish with plain paste, then fill it with uncooked cranberries; add a half-cup of molasses, and four tablespoonfuls of sugar, cover with an upper crust and bake in a quick oven for thirty minutes.

Floating Island

One quart of milk.
Half cup of sugar.
Four eggs.
One teaspoonful of vanilla.
One tablespoonful of cornstarch.

Put the milk on to boil in a farina boiler. Beat the whites of the eggs to a stiff froth, put them, a few spoonfuls at a time, on top of the boiling milk; let cook one minute, and then remove them with a skimmer. Now beat the yolks of the eggs, sugar, and cornstarch together until light, then stir them into the boiling milk; stir until it thickens (about one minute). Take from the fire, add the vanilla, and stand aside to cool. When cold, pour into a glass dish, heap on the whites of the eggs, dot here and there with bits of currant jelly, dust with powdered sugar, and serve very cold.

This will serve eight persons.

"The Bishop goeth
Outlaw hunting"

Boston Cream Cake Pie

Make a Grafton cake and bake it in three layer cake pans. While this is baking, put a quart of milk in a double boiler, add the yolks of four eggs beaten with a half cupful of sugar, stir and cook until it slightly thickens, and pour it, while hot, into the well-beaten whites of the eggs; beat it thoroughly, add a teaspoonful of vanilla and stand aside to cool. At serving time put down a layer of the cake, cover it well with the soft custard, another layer, soft custard, another layer, and pour the remaining custard over the whole. Send to the table immediately.

Any stale cake left over may be served with a soft custard as dessert.

Fruit Shortcake

One pint of Robin Hood flour.
Two level tablespoonfuls of butter or lard.
Two-thirds of a cupful of milk.
Two teaspoonfuls of baking powder.
Half teaspoonful of salt.
Fruit.

Add the baking powder and salt to the flour, sift them, and rub in the butter; add the milk to make a moist, not wet, dough. Roll or pat it into an oblong or square cake, brush the top with milk and bake in a quick oven a half hour. While this is baking, prepare any fresh fruit—peaches (pared), strawberries or raspberries—sweeten them; small fruits should be mashed. When the shortcake is done, pull it into halves, scoop out a portion of the soft crumb and spread both halves with butter. Put the under-half in a platter, heap on a layer of fruit, put on the upper half, garnish it nicely with fruit, dust with sugar and send to the table. Pass with it cream or milk.

Apple Charlotte

Six tart apples.
Half box of gelatin.
One pint of good cream.
Half cupful of powdered sugar.

Pare and quarter the apples, put them in a saucepan with just water enough to prevent burning; when tender, press through a colander, add the sugar and the gelatin, which has been soaked in a half cupful of cold water for a half hour. Stir until the gelatin is dissolved, and pour the mixture into a granite bowl or basin; stand the basin in a pan of cold water or cracked ice to cool. Whip the cream. When the mixture begins to thicken, fold in the cream and turn it once into a pudding mould.

Caution: Stir the mixture while it is cooling, or it will congeal near the ice and give a lumpy appearance to the dessert.

All charlottes may be made after this recipe, using in the place of the apple mixture, orange juice, currant juice, peaches or plums, changing the quantity of sugar to suit the acidity of the fruit.

Coffee Bavarian Cream

Half box of gelatin.
Half pint of milk.
One pint of cream.
One cupful of sugar.
One cupful of strong boiling coffee.
One teaspoonful of vanilla.

Cover the gelatin with cold milk and let it soak for a half hour, then pour into it the boiling coffee, stir over the fire until the gelatin is dissolved, add the sugar, take from the fire, add the vanilla and strain into a tin basin; stir while cooling, and whip the cream. When the mixture begins to thicken fold in the cream, stirring from the bottom and sides of the bowl. Pour into a fancy mould and stand away to harden. Serve plain, or with a garnish of whipped cream.

All Bavarian creams may be made after this recipe. Substitute a pint of made chocolate for the milk and coffee, and you will have Chocolate Bavarian Cream. A pint of mashed strawberries or strawberry juice will give Strawberry Bavarian Cream. Do not heat the fruit juices, but melt the gelatin in a little hot water.

Blanc Mange

One quart of milk.
Six level tablespoonfuls of cornstarch.
Half cupful of sugar.
A teaspoonful of vanilla.
Quarter teaspoonful of salt.

Heat the milk in a double boiler, add the cornstarch, moistened in a little cold milk, and the salt; stir until you have a thick, smooth mass, add the sugar, take from the fire, add the vanilla and pour at once into small custard cups or moulds. Serve cold with sweetened cream.

This may also be served with a sauce of stewed fruit or fruit juices.

Hamburg Cream

Five eggs.
Two lemons.
Half pound of sifted sugar.

Beat the yolks of the eggs with the juice and grated rind of the lemons for fifteen minutes, add the sugar, beat five minutes and stand the bowl in a pan of boiling water; stir constantly until the mixture begins to thicken, then add hastily the well-beaten whites of the eggs. Take from the fire and turn at once into lemonade or dessert glasses. At serving time dust the top with finely chopped nuts or grated macaroons.

South Carolina Snow

Half box of gelatin.
One pint of water.
Half cupful of sugar.
Juice of one lemon.
Whites of three eggs.
One teaspoonful of vanilla.
If you use it, four tablespoonfuls of sherry.

Cover the gelatin with a quarter of a cupful of cold water and let it soak a half hour; add the pint of boiling water, stir until the gelatin is dissolved, add the sugar and all the seasoning, and stand aside until the gelatin is "set," but not hard. Put in the whites of the eggs, unbeaten, and beat the whole until it is as white as snow. Turn into a fancy mould and stand aside to harden. Serve cold, with soft custard made from the yolks of the eggs.

Charlotte Russe

One quart of good cream.
Three-quarter cup of powdered sugar.
One teaspoonful of vanilla.
Half pound of lady fingers.
Half box of gelatin.
Half gill of sherry (if you use wine).

Cover the gelatin with cold water, and let it soak for a half hour. Whip the cream and lay it on a sieve to drain. Line two plain two-quart moulds with the lady fingers. Now turn the cream into a large basin and place it in a pan of cracked ice; add to the soaked gelatin just enough boiling water to dissolve it. Now add the sugar carefully to the cream, then the vanilla and wine, and last, strain in the gelatin. Commence to stir immediately; stir from the sides and bottom of the basin until it begins to thicken, then pour into the moulds and set away on the ice to harden.

Cup Custards

One quart of milk.
Half cup of sugar.
Four eggs.
Quarter of a nutmeg, grated.

Beat the eggs all together until light, then add the sugar, beat again, add the milk and nutmeg, stir until the sugar is dissolved. Pour into custard cups. Stand the cups in a pan of boiling water and then put the pan in the oven. Bake until the custards are set; that is, firm in the centre. When done, take them out of the water and stand away to cool. Serve in the cups.

Angel's Snow

One dozen sweet oranges.
One cup of sugar.
One cocoanut.

Pare and grate the cocoanut. Peel and cut the oranges in small pieces, taking out all the seeds. Put a layer of the oranges in the bottom of a pretty glass dish, sprinkle with sugar, then a layer of cocoanut, then another layer of oranges, sugar, and so on, until the dish is full, having the last layer cocoanut. Let stand one hour, and it is ready to serve.

Baked Custard

Make the same as Cup Custard; pour into a baking dish and bake in a quick oven until firm in the centre. Serve very cold.

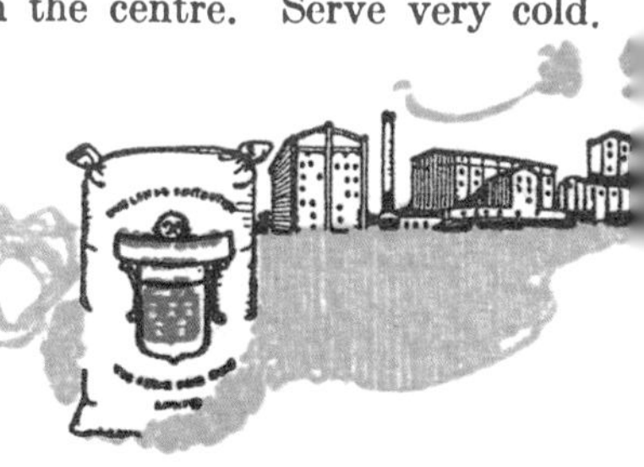

The Sheriff holdeth
a shooting match

Puddings & Sauces

PUDDINGS

Dutch Apple Pudding

Two eggs.
One cupful of milk.
One and a half cupfuls of Robin Hood flour.
Half teaspoonful of salt.
Two teaspoonfuls of baking powder.
Two tablespoonfuls of shortening.
Three good sized apples.

Separate the eggs, beat the yolks, add the milk and the shortening, melted; add the flour and the baking powder, sifted, and the salt, and fold in the well-beaten whites of the eggs. Turn into a shallow baking pan. Have the apples pared, cored and cut into eighths, put them thickly all over the batter, rounding side up, sprinkle over a half cupful of sugar and bake in a quick oven thirty-five to forty minutes. Serve warm, with plain pudding sauce, or milk, or cream.

Peaches, huckleberries or blackberries may be substituted for apples. If well made, this is an exceedingly nice plain pudding.

Mock Charlotte Pudding

One pint of water.
Three level tablespoonfuls of cornstarch.
One cupful of sugar.
One pint of milk.
Four eggs.
One teaspoonful of vanilla.

Moisten the cornstarch with a little cold water, add the pint of boiling water, boil a minute until thick and smooth, add half the sugar, take from the fire and add half the vanilla; pour this, while hot, into the well-beaten whites of the eggs, beating all the while, and turn into a pudding mould to cool. Put the milk over the fire; beat the yolks of the eggs with the remaining sugar, add them to the hot milk, stir until you have a soft custard, take from the fire, add the vanilla and stand aside to cool. Serve the pudding cold in a deep dish, with the sauce poured around.

Bread Pudding

One pint of milk.
One pint of stale bread crumbs.
Two eggs.
A teaspoonful of cinnamon.
Half cupful of sugar.
Half cupful of dried currants or raisins.

Break the bread in pieces, soak it in the milk for fifteen minutes, add the sugar, add all the other ingredients and the eggs, beaten without separating. Bake in a casserole or baking dish until "set" in the middle, about three-quarters of an hour. Serve hot, with plain pudding sauce.

Cottage Pudding

One tablespoonful of butter.
One cupful of sugar.
Half cupful of milk.
Two eggs.
Two rounding teaspoonfuls of baking powder.
One and a quarter cupfuls of Robin Hood flour.

Beat the butter, sugar and the yolks of the eggs together, add the milk, and the flour and baking powder sifted together; beat well and stir in carefully the well-beaten whites of the eggs. Bake in a square cake or bread pan in a moderate oven for three-quarters of an hour. Serve with plain pudding sauce.

Puff Puddings

Two eggs.
One cupful of milk.
Two-thirds of a cupful of Robin Hood flour.
Half teaspoonful of salt.

Beat the eggs without separating until rather light, and add the milk. Add the salt to the flour and gradually stir in the milk and egg; when smooth strain through a sieve and fill into eight hot greased gem pans and bake for three-quarters of an hour until they are light and hollow. Serve hot, with orange sauce.

Puddings and Sauces Continued

Saratoga Pudding

One cupful of molasses.
One cupful of sour milk.
Half pound of raisins.
Half pound of currants.
One teaspoonful of baking soda.
Two and a half cupfuls of Robin Hood flour
Half cupful of chopped suet.
One teaspoonful of cinnamon.
Half nutmeg, grated.
Half teaspoonful of salt.

Mix the suet and molasses. Dissolve the soda in a tablespoonful of warm water, add it to the milk, then add it to the suet and molasses; beat in the flour and spices, add the fruit, well floured, turn the pudding in a pudding bag or mould, and boil continuously for three hours. Allow plenty of room for swelling.

English Plum Pudding

This is the Queen's Two-Guinea Prize Pudding

One pound of seeded raisins.
One pound of suet, chopped fine.
Three-quarters of a pound of stale bread crumbs.
Quarter pound of brown sugar.
One pound of currants.
Quarter pound of Robin Hood flour.
Half nutmeg, grated.
Five eggs.
Half pound of minced candied orange peel.
Half pint of brandy.

Flour the fruit and mix it with all the other dry ingredients. Beat the eggs, add to them the brandy, then pour the mixture over the dry ingredients and mix thoroughly with your hands. Pack into greased small kettles or moulds, or bowls, or bags, and boil ten hours.

This can be done in a fireless cooker, cooking the puddings over night. These will keep for months; simply reheat at serving time.

Queen Mab's Pudding

Half box of gelatin.
One pint of cream.
One pint of milk.
Two-thirds of a cupful of sugar.
Four eggs.
One teaspoonful of vanilla.

Cover the gelatin with a quarter of a cupful of cold water and soak a half hour. Whip the cream. Put the milk over the fire in a double boiler, add the gelatin, stir until the gelatin is dissolved, add the yolks of the eggs and sugar beaten together; when thick like a soft custard, take it from the fire, add the vanilla and turn it in a basin to cool. Stand this in a pan of cracked ice or cold water and stir constantly until it begins to thicken, then stir in carefully the whipped cream; when well mixed, turn into a fancy mould and set away to harden. This may be served plain or with a garnish of whipped cream.

PUDDING SAUCES

Brandy Sauce

Four tablespoonfuls of butter.
Whites of two eggs.
One cupful of powdered sugar.
One gill of boiling water.
One gill of brandy.

Beat the butter and add gradually the sugar; when very light add the whites of the eggs, unbeaten, one at a time; and beat ten minutes. At serving time add the brandy and boiling water, and stand the bowl in a basin of hot water over the fire, stir until light and creamy and use at once.

Hard Sauce

Two level tablespoonfuls of butter.
One cupful of sifted powdered sugar.
The white of an egg.
One teaspoonful of vanilla, or
A tablespoonful of brandy.

Beat the butter to a cream, add gradually the sugar, and when very light drop in the white of an egg; beat until light and frothy, and add the flavoring. Heap into a small dish, dust it lightly with grated nutmeg, and stand on the ice to harden.

Plain Pudding Sauce

Mix two level tablespoonfuls of Robin Hood flour with a half cupful of sugar, add hastily one pint of boiling water and boil a minute; take from the fire, add a tablespoonful of butter and flavor with the grated yellow rind and juice of an orange or lemon, or use vanilla, or sherry.

Sir Richard-of-the-
-Lea repayeth his debt

Ice Cream & Ices

ICE CREAM AND ICES

Directions for Freezing

These directions will answer for the freezing of all ice creams and ices, so that under the recipe simply the word "freeze" will be used. Pound the ice in a large bag with a mallet, or use an ordinary ice shaver. The finer the ice, the less time is required for freezing. A four-quart freezer will require ten pounds of ice and a quart and a pint of coarse rock salt; if finer salt is used one quart will be sufficient.

Put the can in the freezing tub, and adjust the lid and crank; give it a turn before you pack it. Put in a three-inch layer of ice, then a one-inch layer of salt, and so continue until you have the tub filled. Then remove the crank and lid, being careful not to drop salt in the can. Turn in the freezing mixture and re-adjust the top. Turn the crank slowly and steadily until the mixture begins to freeze, then more rapidly until it is completely frozen. If the freezer is properly packed it should take fifteen minutes to freeze the mixture. Too rapid freezing makes the cream coarse and grainy. Too rapid stirring at first makes it buttery.

To Repack the Freezer

Remove the crank, wipe the lid and take it off; remove the dasher, and with a long limber knife or a wooden spoon scrape the cream from the sides of the can; work and pat it down until it is perfectly smooth. Put on the lid, put a cork in the hole in the centre from which the dasher was taken, draw off the water, see that the hole at the side of the freezing tub is open, put over the top a piece of brown paper, then a piece of burlap, and stand it aside for one or two hours to ripen.

Banana Ice Cream

One quart of cream.
Six large bananas.
Half pound of sugar.
One teaspoonful of vanilla.

Put half the cream and all the sugar over the fire in a double boiler; take from the fire and when perfectly cold add the remaining half of the cream. Freeze until the consistency of wet snow, add the bananas (peeled and mashed), turn the crank slowly until the mixture is hard, and repack.

Caramel Ice Cream

One pint of cream.
One pint of milk.
Half pound of sugar.
One teaspoonful of vanilla.
One teaspoonful of maple flavoring.

Scald the milk, add the sugar, take from the fire, add the flavoring, and when perfectly cold add the cream and freeze.

Bisque Ice Cream

One pint of milk.
One quart of cream.
Quarter pound of almond macaroons.
Quarter pound of stale sponge cake.
Four kisses.
One teaspoonful of maple flavoring or caramel.
One teaspoonful of vanilla.
If you use it, four tablespoonfuls of sherry.

Pound the macaroons, kisses and sponge cake through a colander. Put the milk and sugar over the fire; when the sugar is dissolved, add all the flavoring; when cold, add the cream, freeze; when frozen, quite hard, stir in the pounded cake mixture, repack and stand aside to ripen.

Chocolate Ice Cream

One quart of cream.
One pint of milk.
Half pound of sugar.
Four ounces of chocolate.
One teaspoonful of vanilla.
Quarter teaspoonful of cinnamon.

Put the chocolate, grated, in a double boiler with the milk, add the sugar and stir until it reaches the boiling point; take from the fire, add the flavoring, and when perfectly cold add the cream and freeze.

Chocolate ice cream is greatly improved by whipping half the cream and adding it after the mixture is frozen.

Strawberry Ice Cream

One quart of cream.
One full quart of strawberries.
Twelve ounces of sugar.
The juice of one lemon.

Mash the strawberries, add the lemon juice and half the sugar. Put half the cream and the remaining sugar over the fire in a double boiler; when the sugar is dissolved, stand aside to cool; when perfectly cold, add the remaining cream and freeze. When frozen rather stiff, remove the lid, add the mashed berries and continue freezing until the mixture is hard enough to repack.

Raspberries, raspberries and currants, or any small fruit may be substituted for strawberries.

Vanilla Ice Cream

One quart of cream.
Half pound of sugar.
Two teaspoonfuls of vanilla extract.

Heat the sugar with half the cream, take from the fire, add the vanilla, and when cold add the remaining cream and freeze.

The Newest of Creams

One quart of cream.
Half pound of sugar.
One teaspoonful of vanilla.
One teaspoonful of caramel.
One teaspoonful of maple flavoring.
Half pint of chopped black walnut meats.

Heat half the cream with the sugar; when the sugar is dissolved stand aside until very cold, then add the remaining cream, the flavoring and walnuts; freeze.

Frozen Custard

One quart of milk.
The yolks of four eggs.
Half tablespoonful of gelatin.
Two teaspoonfuls of vanilla.
Eight ounces or one cupful of sugar.

Make a soft custard, and when cold, freeze.

Stale brown bread, oatmeal bread, toasted and grated, or stale cake, with a teaspoonful of caramel or maple flavoring, may be added to this after the mixture is frozen.

A little ingenuity will give four or five different ice creams from any one of these recipes.

Coffee Ice Cream

Four ounces of Mocha coffee.
One quart of cream.
Half pound of pulverized sugar.

Have the coffee coarsely ground, put it in a double boiler with half the cream, cover and steep it over the fire for twenty minutes; strain through two thicknesses of cheese cloth, pressing it hard. Add the sugar, stir until it is dissolved, and when cold add the remaining cream and freeze.

Frozen Pudding

Make Frozen Custard, and after you have removed the dasher stir in one cupful of chopped candied fruits, pineapple, gages and cherries.

These creams may be served plain or with sauces.

Hot Chocolate Sauce

Two ounces of chocolate.
One cupful of milk.
One cupful of sugar.
Four tablespoonfuls of water.
One teaspoonful of vanilla.

Put the chocolate and water over the fire; and when the chocolate is melted add the sugar and the milk; stir constantly and boil until you have a sauce that is the consistency of thick cream. Serve at once.

Nut Sauce

Boil one cupful of sugar with a half cupful of water and a tablespoonful of lemon juice to the thickness of cream; take from the fire, add a teaspoonful of maple flavoring or caramel, and a quarter of a cupful of chopped nuts. Serve cold.

Orange Water Ice

Twelve large oranges.
One pound of sugar.
One quart of water.

Add the sugar to the water, add the yellow grated rind of three oranges, boil five minutes and strain; when perfectly cold add the juice of the oranges and freeze.

Lemon water ice may be made after this recipe, using four large lemons to a quart of water and a pound and a quarter of sugar.

All fruit juices, and grated pineapple, may be sweetened to taste and frozen.

These are also called sorbet or sherbet.

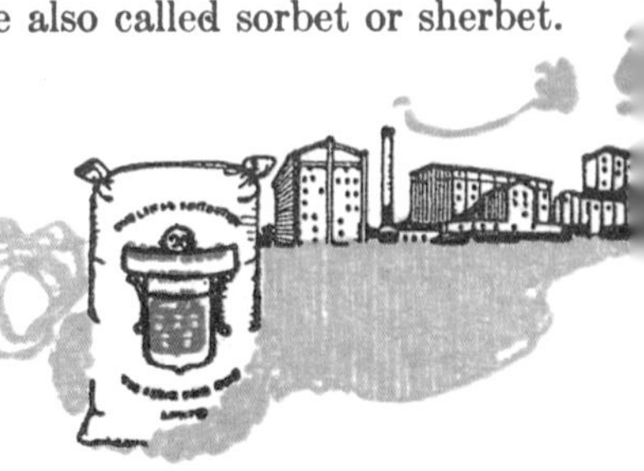

LONDON
"King Richard cometh
to Sherwood Forest"

Bev-
erages

BEVERAGES

Water alone fulfils the place of a true beverage. Tea and coffee, when saturated with sugar and cream, are certainly light, stimulating foods, and chocolate is quite a concentrated liquid food. A cup of good chocolate, with a slice of bread and butter, make an excellent breakfast for a school child.

Coffee

A perfect infusion of the coffee berry is made by simply pouring boiling water over finely ground, well-roasted coffee, allowing three rounding tablespoonfuls to each pint of water. Scald the percolator, which may be either tin, copper or glass; pour out the water, put in the desired quantity of coffee and pour over it the given quantity of water. If the coffee is not sufficiently strong, draw it off and pour it over the grounds again. I prefer a percolator with an alcohol lamp underneath; the water may then be boiled in the pot and sent up through a tube to spray itself down over the coffee. Five minutes' boiling makes good coffee, and the grounds are always above the water. This is a point to be remembered; that any method of making coffee where the grounds are in the water is objectionable; it spoils the flavor of the very best of coffee.

There are a number of good cheap pots in the market that hold the grounds above the water and make good coffee.

The coffee must not be powdered or the infusion will be muddy.

Boiled Coffee

Allow a rounding tablespoonful of coffee to each cupful of water. Put the coffee in an ordinary coffee pot, drop in a little white of egg, and sufficient cold water to moisten; stir, then pour on the given quantity of boiling water. Bring quickly to boiling point, lift from the fire a minute, put it back, bring again to boiling point, lift it up, and bring it the third time to boiling point; this time let it boil rapidly just a minute, take from the fire, add a little cold water and stand aside to settle. Draw this off into a hot china pot; heat the pot by pouring in boiling water.

Café au Lait or Breakfast Coffee

This is made according to the first recipe. To serve, fill the breakfast cup half full of hot, not boiled, milk, and draw in the strong coffee.

Tea

First of all, select good tea. No matter what kind you buy, the making is always the same. Use a china pot and scald it; pour out the water and put into the hot pot a level teaspoonful of good tea to each pint of water. If the water is soft, take it at the first boil; if hard, boil it ten minutes. Cover the pot with a cozy and let it stand for five minutes.

Caution: Tea must not be made over the fire, nor should it be made in a metal pot. To have a perfectly wholesome infusion, it must be drawn carefully and used at once.

Chocolate

Chocolate and cocoa both contain starch, hence they must be boiled. Allow a quarter of a pound of chocolate to each quart and a pint of milk and a pint of water, with

Half cupful of sugar,
A teaspoonful of vanilla,
One level tablespoonful of cornstarch.

Grate the chocolate, add the water and sugar; stir and boil for five minutes. Heat the milk in a double boiler; add the cornstarch, moistened in a little cold milk, cook to the consistency of thin cream; add the chocolate, cover the boiler and let the water surrounding it boil rapidly five minutes, beat rapidly with an egg-beater, take from the fire and add the vanilla.

Serve plain or with whipped cream.

Beverages Continued

West Indian Cocoa

Four tablespoonfuls of cocoa.
Half a vanilla bean, or a teaspoonful of vanilla extract.
Half cupful of sugar.
A saltspoonful of cinnamon.
Half pint of water.
One quart of milk.
One level tablespoonful of cornstarch.

Put the milk in a double boiler, when hot add the cornstarch and the vanilla bean (cut into bits); stir until the thickness of thin cream. Put the sugar, cocoa and water in a saucepan, stir and boil for five minutes, add this to the hot milk, cook and stir for five minutes longer, whip with an egg-beater and serve with whipped cream on each cup.

East Indian Punch

Make a strong tea, using double quantity of tea; strain and add to each quart the juice of two lemons and one orange, and sufficient sugar to sweeten. At serving time pour this into the punch bowl over a block of ice, and add sufficient Apollinaris to make it palatable. If Apollinaris is not to be had, ginger ale or bottled soda water will answer.

Wedding Punch

One tumbler of currant jelly.
One tumbler of raspberry jelly or jam.
One tumbler of blackberry jelly or jam.
Twelve lemons.
Two oranges.
One pint of grape juice.
Four bottles of ginger ale.
Three quart bottles of Apollinaris.
One bottle of sarsaparilla.
One pint of grated pineapple.
One pint of preserved strawberries.
One quart can of peaches.
Two pounds of sugar.

Grate the yellow rind from the oranges and lemons into the sugar; put this in the preserving kettle, add one quart of water, and when the sugar is dissolved boil ten minutes, without stirring; strain while hot, add all the jellies and fruits, and stand aside to cool. When cool, strain through a colander, cover and stand aside over night. At serving time add the grape juice, the juice of the oranges and lemons, and the sarsaparilla. Put a block of ice, or one quart of shaved ice in the punch bowl, add a sufficient quantity of the punch, a bottle of ginger ale and a quart of Apollinaris. When this is consumed, put in more punch, more ginger ale and more Apollinaris. Or, if you like, you may mix the ginger ale and Apollinaris with the other ingredients, and then fill the punch bowl, as needed.

Cocoa

Put one quart of milk to boil in a farina boiler. Moisten four tablespoonfuls of cocoa with a little cold milk, pour it into the boiling milk, stirring all the while. Stir until it comes to boiling-point, cover the farina boiler, and boil five minutes. Serve with whipped cream.

Broma, alkathrepta, and racahout are all made precisely the same as Cocoa.

Cocoa From the Nibs

Put a half-cup of the broken cocoa into a farina boiler with two quarts of boiling water. Boil two hours, or until reduced to one quart, then add one pint of boiling cream, and serve.

Racahout Powder

One pound of rice flour.
One pound of confectioner's XXX sugar.
One ounce of powdered salep.
One pound of cocoa.
Two ounces of arrowroot.
Two ounces of sugar of milk.
One vanilla bean.

Mix and thoroughly rub together, put into glass jars, and fasten.

Raspberry Vinegar

Put two quarts of raspberries into a stone jar, and pour over them one quart of good cider vinegar. Cover and stand aside for two days, then drain off the liquid without mashing the berries, pour it over a quart of fresh fruit, and stand as before. Do this once more, the last time straining through a muslin bag. Now add one pound of sugar to every pint of this liquid. Boil slowly five minutes, skim, let stand fifteen minutes, bottle and seal.

Strawberry and blackberry vinegars are made in precisely the same manner.

"Robin Hood and Maid Marian are wed"

JELLIES, PRESERVES AND CANNING

Directions for Canning

Fruits may be canned by cooking them in the jars, or they may be cooked in a porcelain kettle, and then put carefully into the jars. The first method is the better. Fill the jars with the fruit, cover with cold syrup, adjust the rubbers, put on the lids loosely, stand them in a wash boiler, the bottom of which is protected with a rack, surround them partly with cold water, bring to boiling point, boil twenty minutes, screw on the tops and stand them aside. Use more or less sugar, according to the acidity of the fruit

Canned Peaches

Pare the peaches, cut them into halves and put them in a bowl of cold water to prevent discoloration. To each pound allow a quarter of a pound of sugar and a half pint of water. Boil the sugar and water, put the peaches in the jars, fill the jars to overflowing with the syrup and finish as directed. Peaches may be boiled fifteen, twenty or twenty-five minutes.

To Preserve Peaches

Pare the peaches, weigh them and to each pound allow three-quarters of a pound of sugar and a pint of water. Boil the sugar and water, add a little cream of tartar or lemon juice, add the peaches to the hot syrup, cook slowly until transparent, put them in jars or tumblers and when cold, seal.

Wiesbaden Strawberries

Stem six quarts of sound, quite red strawberries. Put them in a colander and wash by plunging the colander down into cold water Weigh the strawberries, and to each pound allow a pound of sugar. Put a layer of strawberries and a layer of sugar in the preserving kettle, cover and stand aside over night. Next morning drain the juice from the berries, pressing them lightly. Have ready six quarts of the finest berries that you can find in the market; wash them if necessary, stem and put them in glass jars or tumblers. Boil the strawberry syrup carefully for twenty minutes, skimming until it is perfectly clear. Test it every now and then to see if it will form a jelly if cold. Fill the jars with this boiling syrup, adjust the rubbers and tops that have been thoroughly scalded, put the jars on their sides in a wash boiler, the bottom of which is protected, cover with boiling water and boil rapidly fifteen minutes. Take them from the boiler and stand them outside in the hot sun; as the sun goes down bring them in, and put them out the next day and the next.

It is wise to use half pint or pint jars for all fine preserved fruits.

Bar-le-Duc

Wash large white currants and remove them from the stems; put a layer in the bottom of the preserving kettle, pour over sufficient boiling strained honey to cover, and stand aside for twenty-four hours. Next morning lift the currants with a skimmer and put them in small tumblers. Boil the syrup until thick (about ten minutes), fill the tumblers, cover with paraffin and stand aside.

Red currants may be used in the place of white.

Orange Marmalade

Take equal weights of Seville oranges and sugar, cut them into thin slices toward the core; cover with six quarts of cold water and stand aside for twenty-four hours. Then boil carefully for three hours, add seven pounds of white sugar and boil until clear and jelly-like.

One may take ordinary oranges and add one grape fruit and two lemons to each dozen.

Gooseberry Jam

Mix two quarts of ripe and two quarts of green gooseberries. Top and tail them, put them in your preserving kettle with just enough water to prevent scorching. Boil and stir twenty minutes, then add half the quantity of sugar, boil ten minutes longer and put away in jam pots.

Carrot Marmalade

Wash, scrape and grate two pounds of full grown carrots; add an equal quantity of ripe pared peaches or apricots. Measure the mixture, and to each pint allow a half pint of sugar. Put the carrot mixture in the preserving kettle, stir constantly until it reaches the boiling point, cook slowly twenty minutes, add the sugar and the juice of one lemon, and boil slowly until transparent.

Canned Tomatoes, Whole

Peel solid small tomatoes, pack them in wide-mouthed jars, add a teaspoonful of salt to each jar and fill them to overflowing with cold water. Adjust the rubbers, put the lids on loosely, stand them in a wash boiler, surround them with cold water, bring to boiling point and boil rapidly for three minutes; then fasten the tops quickly and stand them aside.

If these tomatoes are soft, the cooking has been too long.

Jelly Making

Try to become familiar with the character and peculiarities of fruit and sugar before attempting to make perfect jelly. Good granulated sugar and fruit just ripe and freshly picked are necessary. After fruit becomes dead ripe, or after it stands for a short time, there is a chemical change which makes it difficult to get a firm, clear, solid jelly.

Cane sugar boiled with acid fruits is very apt to "split," and divide into two sugars, one levulose and the other dextrose, neither of which make a firm jelly. This fact tells you to boil the juice before adding the sugar.

Among the fruits that are quite easily made into jelly are crabapples, guavas, under-ripe or just ripe grapes, apples, under-ripe blackberries, and quinces. They yield a very stiff jelly, using only a half pound of sugar to each pint of juice. Large fruits, like quinces, apples and crabapples, need not be pared, but the seeds and seed vesicles must be removed.

Crabapple Jelly

Remove the seeds and cores, cut the fruit into quarters or strips, put it in a porcelain lined kettle and cover with cold water, allowing to each pound of fruit one pint of water. Cover the kettle, boil and stir thirty minutes, turn the pulp into a jelly bag and let it drain over night. Next morning measure the liquor and to each pint allow a half pound of sugar. Put the sugar in a large baking pan and stand it in the oven to warm. Put the liquor into the preserving kettle, boil rapidly twenty minutes, add the sugar, stir until the sugar is dissolved, bring again to a boil, and nine out of ten times it will jelly instantly. Try by taking a teaspoonful or two out into a saucer and placing it in a cold place; if it solidifies on the surface, and drops, rather than pours, from the spoon, it is ready to put into the tumblers. When the jelly is cold cover it with a thin layer of paraffin, then cover the tops with papers and stand in a cool, light place for keeping. I frequently wet the tops of the papers with a little white of egg and water, using a soft brush; when they dry they tighten and form a very good covering.

Small Fruits

Blackberries, raspberries, currants and strawberries may be mashed and the juice strained and boiled without water.

Add just a little water to grapes to prevent scorching. Cook them fifteen to twenty minutes, mash them and drain. Next day measure the liquor, allow a pound of sugar to each pint of juice, and finish the same as crabapple jelly.

Use as little water as possible for plums, and finish the same as crabapple jelly.

Elderberries, cherries, peaches, pears and huckleberries must be mixed with an equal quantity of green grapes or crab-apples to make a perfectly good, stiff jelly.

"Robin Hood shooteth
his last shaft"

Instructions & Measures

Table of Weights and Measures

To save confusion in weights and measurements, level all measurements. Wherever a tablespoonful is mentioned it means a level tablespoonful. Where a cupful is mentioned it means the ordinary cooking-school cup, which holds an exact half-pint.

4 teaspoonfuls of liquid	equals	1 tablespoonful.
4 tablespoonfuls of liquid	"	½ gill, ¼ cup, or 1 wineglassful.
1 tablespoonful of liquid	"	½ ounce.
1 pint of liquid	"	1 pound.
2 gills of liquid	"	1 cup or ½ pint.
1 kitchen cup	"	½ pint.
1 quart of sifted flour	"	1 pound.
4 cups of flour	"	1 qt. or 1 pound.
2 tablespoonfuls of flour	"	½ ounce.
3 cups of corn meal	"	1 pound.
1½ pints of corn meal	"	1 pound.
1 cup of butter	"	½ pound.
1 pint of butter	"	1 pound.
1 tablespoonful of butter	"	½ ounce.
1 solid pint of chopped meat	"	1 pound.
10 eggs	"	1 pound.
2 cupfuls of granulated sugar	"	1 pound.
1 pint of granulated sugar	"	1 pound.
1 pint of brown sugar	"	13 ounces.
2½ cups of powdered sugar	"	1 pound.

Kitchen Calendar

A medium sized potato will bake in three-quarters of an hour at a temperature of 300° Fahrenheit; at high altitude it will always take ten to fifteen minutes longer.

In boiling meats, immerse the meat in boiling water, boil rapidly for five minutes and cook slowly at a temperature of 180° Fahrenheit, twenty minutes to each pound; or in a fireless cooker over night.

An eight-pound turkey, stuffed, will require an oven of 400° Fahrenheit for three hours; without stuffing, two and a half hours.

A four-pound chicken, with stuffing, will require, at a temperature of 400° Fahrenheit, two hours.

A tame duck one year old, stuffed with potatoes, will require two and a half hours at a temperature of 360° Fahrenheit.

A young goose, stuffed, three hours at a temperature of 360° Fahrenheit.

Oysters are done when the gills curl.

Game, such as woodcock, snipe and pheasants, must be roasted in a hot oven, about 400° Fahrenheit, forty-five minutes.

Partridges, split down the back, will bake in forty minutes in a hot oven.

Prairie chickens, forty-five minutes, at 400° Fahrenheit.

A haunch of venison will cook in a quick oven (400° Fahrenheit) two and a half hours to three hours, basting frequently. Serve rare.

To test meats, run a skewer in the fleshy part; if blood follows and is a dark red, cook longer; if the blood is mixed with juice and is slightly pink, it is done.

Serve all red meats rare; white meats, well done.

All meats must go into a very hot oven at first; after they have been thoroughly seared, cool the oven and cook slowly.

Bread, in square loaves, must be baked at 360° Fahrenheit for forty minutes.

Pastry requires a very hot oven, and must be baked until light.

Muffins, gems and small breads must be baked in a quick oven twenty minutes to a half hour.

Custard pies must have a strong under-heat, or the under crust will be soggy.

These temperatures are given for ordinary coal stoves; if gas is used allow 20° less than the temperature given.

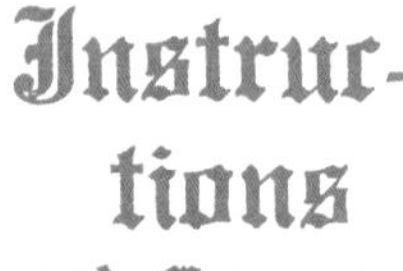

Time Required at Sea Level for Cooking Green Vegetables

At an altitude of three or four thousand feet the time must be increased for most vegetables; old beans, peas, lentils, rice and macaroni should be cooked in a fireless cooker; this will save both time and trouble, and make the food much more palatable.

Green peas, young and fresh	15	minutes
Green peas, old and not fresh	30	"
String beans	45	"
Beans, shelled (green)	45	"
Lima beans, young, fresh	30	"
Lima beans, dried (soaked)	45	"
Cabbage, whole head, simmer	2	hours
Cabbage, half head	1	hour
Cabbage, quarter head	30	minutes
Cabbage, chopped	20	"
Cauliflower and Broccoli	30	"
Cucumbers, cut into quarters	30	"
Squash, pared and cut into blocks	20	"
Pumpkin, in squares for pies	30	"
Tomatoes, peeled and stewed	30	"
Tomatoes, baked, whole, slow oven	1	hour
Tomatoes, stuffed and baked	1	"
Green peppers, stuffed	1	"
Green peppers, stewed	30	minutes
Onions, new	45	"
Spanish onions, whole	2	hours
Spanish onions, cut into slices	1	hour
Okra	1	"
Celery, stewed	30	minutes
Spinach	10	"
Brussels Sprouts, fresh	30	"
Kale	45	"
Bananas, baked (240°)	30	"
Apples, sweet, baked (slow)	30	"
Apples, sour, baked (slow)	20	"

To Clarify Fat

A careful cook seldom buys lard; she saves all the skimming from soup, all trimmings from steaks, and the dripping from roasts. Put the dripping to be clarified into a saucepan, set it over a moderate fire until all the fat is melted; then strain into a clean pan, and add to every three pounds of this fat a pint of boiling water and a quarter teaspoonful of baking soda. Stand over a moderate fire and boil until the water has evaporated and the fat is clear. Skim, strain through a fine sieve into a tin kettle, and it is ready to use.

To Scald Milk

Put the milk in a basin or farina boiler, stand it in a pan of boiling water over the fire, and as soon as the milk begins to steam it is scalded.

Rule For Cooking Dry and Underground Vegetables

All underground vegetables are, as a rule, rich in woody fibre; use boiling, unsalted water to start, adding salt when they are partly cooked.

Potatoes, to boil until they can be easily pierced to the centre with a fork	30	minutes
Potatoes, to bake, slowly	45	"
Potatoes, cut into dice to cream	10	"
Rice, Carolina	30	"
Rice, Patna	20	"
Beans, soup, dried, soaked over night, slowly	2	hours
Beans, if for baking, until skin cracks	30	minutes
Peas, dried, soaked over night	2	hours
Lentils, dried, soaked over night	1	hour
Sweet potatoes, medium size, to boil	40	minutes
Sweet potatoes, medium size, to bake	45-50	"
Turnips, white, cut into blocks, to stew	20	"
Turnips, yellow, cut into blocks, to stew	30	"
Carrots, cut into dice, to stew	1	hour
Parsnips, cut into halves	1	"
Beets, new	45	minutes
Beets, old	4	hours
Salsify, boiled	45	minutes
Globe artichokes	45	"
Jerusalem artichokes, sliced	30	"
Jerusalem artichokes, whole	45	"
Asparagus	45	"
Polk shoots	45	"
Green sweet corn, after it begins to boil	5	"

To Make a Jelly-Bag

Take one yard of thick all-wool flannel, fold the two opposite corners together, fell the side, making a triangular bag. Bind the top with heavy tape, and fasten on the upper side two or three heavy loops by which it may be hung up.

To Salt Almonds

Shell, blanch and spread them out on a bright tin pie dish, add a piece of butter the size of a hickory-nut, and stand them in a moderate oven until a golden brown. Take them from the oven, stir them around, dredge them thickly with salt, and turn out to cool.

To Blanch Almonds

Shell them, throw them into boiling water, and let stand on the back part of the stove five minutes, then throw them into cold water, and rub them between the hands to remove the skins.

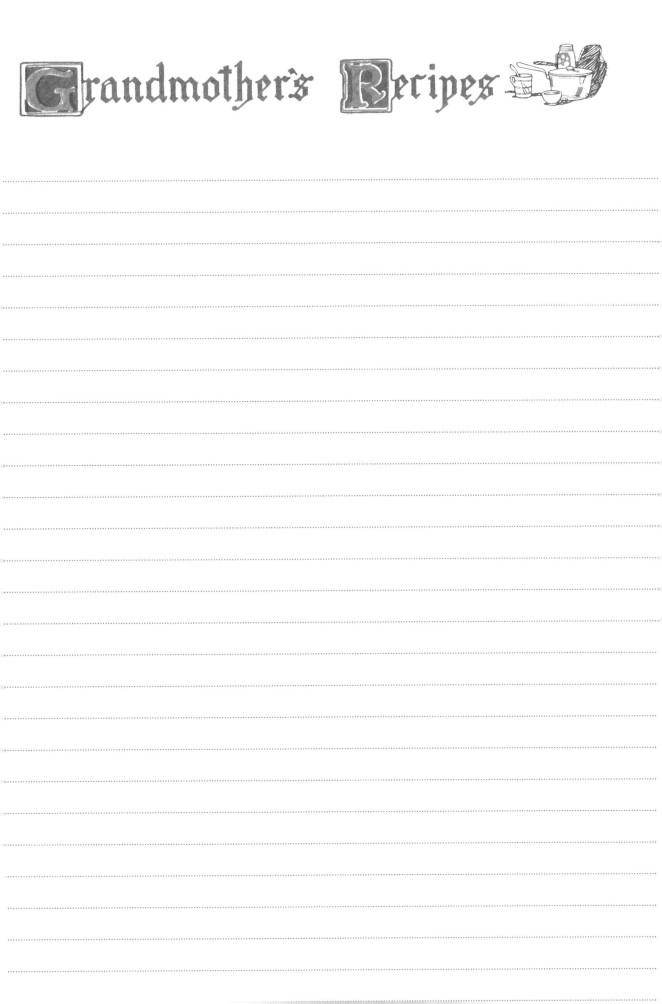
Grandmother's Recipes

Mother's Recipes

Aunties Recipes

Historical Notes

by Elizabeth Driver

The first barrels of Robin Hood Flour rolled out of a mill in Moose Jaw, Saskatchewan, in 1909, in a period when new immigrants were flooding into the wheat plains of Western Canada. Robin Hood was one of four brands created that year by Saskatchewan Flour Mills Co. Ltd, a new company formed by Francis Atherton Bean, the American owner of International Milling Co. in New Prague, Minnesota.[1] Whereas the American parent company focussed on flour for commercial baking until after World War II, the growth of the Canadian business was fuelled, from the very beginning, by the vigorous promotion of its domestic brand, Robin Hood, across Canada. In 1912, just three years after the launch of Robin Hood Flour, Bean renamed the firm after the brand, and a few years later, in about 1915,[2] Robin Hood Mills Ltd published *Robin Hood Flour Cook Book*, its first advertising recipe collection. Today, Robin Hood Multifoods Inc. is a public company that sells many types of product, from flour and baking mixes to pickles and dog food, but it is still named after the famous Robin Hood brand conceived in Moose Jaw almost a hundred years ago.

A Cookbook "Worthy of the Robin Hood Name"

Bean's plans for Robin Hood Flour were ambitious and the company employed a variety of strategies to establish the brand in the Canadian marketplace – even, in 1912, trumpeting the merits of the flour from a sign on a circus elephant.[3] Advertising cookbooks were popular with the public, but how might one from Robin Hood Mills stand out from others, especially those published by competitors, such as *Ogilvie's Book for a Cook* of 1905 and *Five Roses Cook Book* of 1913?[4] As the Foreword to the *Robin Hood Flour Cook Book* explains, the company aimed to produce a book "worthy of the Robin Hood name" and "different." Nearly two years of work and $10,000 went into the project.

Mr. L. Moen,[5] a "leading American artist," prepared seven colour plates and forty illustrations. At the top of the recipe pages, his drawings tell the story of Robin Hood; at the bottom, art-nouveau swirls connect medieval food scenes with modern vignettes of the Moose Jaw mill, fields of prairie wheat, and sacks of Robin Hood Flour. One especially pleasing coincidence of drawing and text is on page 15, where the image of "Robin Hood turneth butcher" decorates the opening of the "Meats" chapter. Work on the *Robin Hood Flour Cook Book* likely started about the time that the *Five Roses Cook Book* was published, but the quality of the artwork and graphic design of the Robin Hood volume surpasses that of its predecessor by every measure.

To write the text, Robin Hood Mills commissioned (in the words of the Foreword) "the best recognized authority on the culinary art," Sarah Tyson Rorer, née Heston (1849–1937). A well-known author distinguished the Robin Hood cookbook from the Ogilvie and Five Roses ones, which were anonymous compilations of recipes from several sources. The Philadelphia-based Mrs. Rorer was a natural choice for an American-owned company, and there were no Canadian cooks of comparable fame at the time (although Canada would produce its own national cooking celebrities over the next few decades).

Mrs. Rorer, Culinary Star

When Mrs. Rorer wrote the *Robin Hood Flour Cook Book*, she was already in her mid-sixties and renowned throughout North America as a prolific author of about forty cookbooks, a charismatic and witty lecturer and demonstrator, founder and Principal of the Philadelphia School of Cookery from 1884 to 1903, and past editor of the *Ladies' Home Journal*.[6] Over her long career, huge numbers of women had attended her travelling cooking schools, including nearly a quarter of a million people during the Chicago World's Fair in 1893! In March 1898, she drew an enthusiastic audience of Canadian women to a series of lectures at the London, Ontario,

Y.M.C.A., news of which was widely reported in the *Farmer's Advocate* of 15 April 1898, along with a selection of her recipes. Her cookbooks were sold in Canadian bookstores, either the original American editions[7] or, in a few cases, Canadian editions of the American works, notably *Mrs. Rorer's New Cook Book* (Toronto: The Musson Book Co. Ltd, [February 1903]); and some of her recipes appeared in French- and English-language Montreal editions of advertising cookbooks for an American shortening called Cottolene. It was a coup for Robin Hood Mills to secure Mrs. Rorer as an author, and the fee paid for her service was "handsome." The *Robin Hood Flour Cook Book* is the only cookbook by this American writer that was created exclusively for the Canadian market and that promoted Canadian food products. By employing Mrs. Rorer and printing her name on the front cover, Robin Hood Mills surely hoped she would boost the profile of its Robin Hood brand in the eyes of the Canadian public.

The Recipes

For the Robin Hood text, Mrs. Rorer drew upon material she had collected over many years. Not surprisingly, the organization of the chapters, the selection of recipes, and the phrasing of the instructions show many parallels with her massive, 731-page reference work, *Mrs. Rorer's New Cook Book*, first published in Philadelphia in 1902, and itself an accumulation of twenty years' experience. Sometimes the wording in the Robin Hood book is virtually identical to that in *Mrs. Rorer's New Cook Book*, for example, the recipes for Home Made Yeast and for English Plum Pudding. Often, the instructions for the same recipe are abbreviated and simplified, such as in the case of Chicken Croquettes, where the Robin Hood text specifies cooked-and-chopped chicken, instead of explaining the full process of boiling the bird. In other instances, Mrs. Rorer recast two recipes from her *New Cook Book* as one recipe: Cream of Green Pea Soup and Cream of Pea Soup from Canned Peas became Cream of Pea Soup, incorporating directions for both fresh and canned peas.

Although the *Robin Hood Flour Cook Book* contains only 78 pages, Mrs. Rorer offered a wide variety of recipes, from sophisticated and elegant items, such as Chicken in Jelly ("a beautiful dish to serve for afternoon receptions"), to the humblest meal of Oatmeal Gruel ("an exceedingly nice food for children or for the aged").

There are many distinctly American recipe names (Eggs Jefferson, South Carolina Snow, Saratoga Pudding), but also recipes from other national cuisines (Baked Ribs of Beef with Yorkshire Pudding, from England; Sauce Bechamel, from France; Egg Plant, West Indian Style; Frijoles, from Mexico). Canadians, particularly those in rural areas, would have appreciated her inclusion of recipes for venison, rabbit, wild ducks and goose, partridge and bear, and prairie chickens, and that she acknowledged the different cooking technologies in use at the time (she tells, for example, how to cook planked fish in front of a wood fire, under the flames of a gas stove, or in a coal-stove oven; and she suggests fireless cookers as an alternative for Tournedos).

Mrs. Rorer's selection was generally familiar to Canadian home cooks, yet the absence of certain recipes revealed her American origin. Canadian families traditionally enjoyed baked goods and puddings made with dried fruit, especially raisins and currants. The *Robin Hood Flour Cook Book* has only one recipe for Plum Pudding and one for Mince Pie, whereas the *Five Roses Cook Book*, compiled from recipes submitted by over two thousand Canadians, has three versions of Plum Pudding, three Christmas Puddings, three Carrot Puddings (a popular lighter variation featuring grated potato and grated carrot), four Mince Pies, six Fruit Cakes, and two Christmas Cakes. Also in the Five Roses text, but missing from the Robin Hood collection, are Butter Tarts, Maple Syrup Tarts, and Maple Syrup Pie. A whole chapter in the Five Roses book is devoted to "Doughnuts, Crullers, and Other Fried Cakes"; Mrs. Rorer omitted doughnuts altogether. Canadians may have missed these and a few other favourite recipes from their standard repertoire, but they would have appreciated the scope of Mrs. Rorer's collection, perhaps savoured some new and unfamiliar dishes, and found her instructions clear and reliable.

* * *

The *Robin Hood Flour Cook Book* was undoubtedly treasured as a useful and attractive companion in the kitchen. Many years after its first publication, the company received a letter dated 30 September 1931, from Mrs. G.B. Thrasher of Bull River, British Columbia.[8] In the letter, Mrs. Thrasher, a loyal user of Robin Hood Flour since 1914, told of the tragic loss of all her belongings in a forest fire. In a testament to the value of the *Robin Hood Flour Cook Book*, she requested another copy as she was "utterly at a loss without it now after using it in so many years."

End Notes

Historical Notes

1. The other three brands were Radium, Keynote, and Saskania. For a contemporary report of the opening of the plant, see "Saskatchewan Flour Mills Opened To-Day," *Moose Jaw Evening Times* 27 January 1909, pp. 1, 3.

2. The only date printed in the book – 1914 – appears on the container of Robin Hood Porridge Wheat depicted on p. 35, and it is the copyright year for the product name; however, the volume belonging to the Elrose Heritage Society in Elrose, Saskatchewan, is identified as "brought by Mrs. Adam Kelsey to the homestead in 1915."

3. "Speaking of Our Products," *Grist* [in-house magazine] Vol. 23, No. 2 (75th Anniversary Issue, 1967): p. 3.

4. *Ogilvie's Book for a Cook* of 1905 and the 1915 edition of *Five Roses Cook Book* are available in facsimile reprints by Whitecap Books.

5. His monogram, L.M., is visible in many of the drawings.

6. For an account of Mrs. Rorer's career and her magnetic personality, see Emma Seifrit Weigley, "The Philadelphia Chef: Mastering the Art of Philadelphia Cookery," *Philadelphia Magazine of History and Biography* Vol. 96, No. 2 (April 1972): pp. 229–40.

7. See, for example, entries in the Stock Books of the Methodist Book and Publishing House in Toronto, held at the United Church of Canada and Victoria University Archives (Acc. 83.061C, UCC Board of Publication, Series III, Box 39): Stock Book 1909, p. 49, lists "11 [copies] Mrs Orers[*sic*] Best Riceps[*sic*]"; an entry for "3 [copies] Canning and Preserving," under "Public Schools" on p. 170, may also refer to a Rorer title.

8. Printed in *Grist* (January 1932): p 18.